Los Gatos Observed

By Alastair Dallas

With Mary Tomasi-Dubois

Photographs by Peter S. Conrad

infospect press
Los Gatos, California

Los Gatos Observed

NOTE
Please observe Los Gatos with respect for the owners and occupants of the beautiful homes and buildings listed herein.

PUBLISHED BY
Infospect Press
17681 Foster Road
Los Gatos, California 95030-7154
http://www.losgatosobserved.com

Dallas, Alastair.
    Los Gatos Observed / Alastair Dallas with Mary Tomasi-Dubois. Photographs by Peter S. Conrad.
        p.192   cm.
    Includes index.
    ISBN 0-9670268-0-6
        1. Architecture-California-Los Gatos-Guidebooks. 2. Los Gatos (Ca.)-History. 3. Los Gatos (Ca.)-Buildings, structures, etc.-Guidebooks. I. Dallas, Alastair, 1957-. II. Tomasi-Dubois, Mary, 1943-. III. Conrad, Peter S., 1968-.

Printed and bound in the United States of America on acid-free paper.

1 2 3 4 5 6 7 8 9 MLML 4 9 8 7 6 5

Book design by Peggy Maloney and Tom Parker.

Table of Contents

Acknowledgements

HISTORY REPEATS ITSELF; historians repeat each other. We must therefore start by acknowledging our debt to those who collected and preserved and presented Los Gatos for the ages.

The history of Los Gatos has been preserved by generations of volunteers. We are grateful to Clarence F. Hamsher, of the First National Bank, who collected photographs and newspaper clippings and, more than anyone, allowed the town's heritage to survive the Dark Ages when building new meant destroying the old. And, of course, to Dr. George Bruntz, history teacher at Los Gatos High School and later professor at San Jose State, who wrote *The History of Los Gatos, Gem City of the Foothills,* based in part on Hamsher's research. Hamsher's clippings were carefully mounted, bound and indexed by countless volunteers to aid Dr. Bruntz and the materials are still available at the library.

The Town staff and library have maintained a wealth of information down through the years, particularly including property tax records, town directories and phone books, and a bound set of Sanborn fire insurance maps showing every structure in town as of specific dates. The Museum Association at the Forbes Mill Annex also has a trove of data. More than any other resource, we are grateful for the inventory which the town commissioned from San Francisco-based architectural historian Anne Bloomfield around the time of the 1989 earthquake.

WILLIAM A. WULF, Los Gatos Historian, has collected an extensive library of books, photographs and memorabilia.

Los Gatos is well-served by several amateur historians, each of whom graciously shared their knowledge for this book: Pat Dunning, Wilma Thompson, and William Wulf. Bill Wulf, the town's official historian, knows more than anyone else ever will about the town, its people, and their customs and history, and he has been irrationally generous with his time and historical materials over the years. He began, as a high school student, by transcribing the correspondence of James Forbes, and he has contributed several well-researched pieces to the library's collection. In 1978, he persuaded the U. S. Geological Survey to rename the ridge on the Santa Cruz county line "Cuesta de Los Gatos," restoring its traditional name. Owing to his life-long fascination with trains, he has collected memorabilia such as a conductor's cap or a ticket punch from the interurban line. He has an extensive library and many one-of-a-kind photographs. If this book inspires you regarding the history of Los Gatos, thank Bill Wulf, because he inspired the authors.

Confucius said, "Study the past if you would divine the future." Henry Ford, on the other hand, said, shortly after his visit to Los Gatos in 1915, "History, more or less, is bunk. We want to live in the present and the only history that is worth a tinker's damn is the history we make today." This book is intended as an aid to understanding and appreciating the past in order that we each may make the best of history today for ourselves and our community.

Before commencing, however, there are many people to thank. This book began with Mary Tomasi-Dubois' concept and it has only taken off with her assistance and encouragement. And as those of you who know her will attest, Kathryn Morgan knows enough about Los Gatos to write several books herself, so the complimentary words in her Introduction are high praise, indeed. Although I take responsibility for all remaining errors, I'd also like to thank Mary, Kathryn, my wife Peggy Dallas and my mother Dorothea Dallas for carefully examining draft after draft for errors of all kinds.

Thanks for making their homes available: Thomas & Ann Atkinson; Dr. R. Laurence Berkowitz; Peter & Dennise Carter; Audrey & Bob Christianson; Suzanne & Clark Cochran; Wendy & Richard Fox; Roberta Fries; Floyd & Leilani Frisch; Isabel Gibbs; Brian Hinman; Vasliki Kidder; Michael Krolak; Andre & Jean Libante; Alex Lunginovic; James & Brenda Lyon; Scotty McEwen; Dr. Jamal Modir; Allan & Anne Morton; Pamela Maudlin & Tim Murphy; Catherine & John Petrek; Judge Melinda Jane Stewart; Lucille & Stan Switzer; Irene & Thomas Upson; Susan & Tom Ward; Mike & Kim Wasserman; Kathleen Watson; Terri & John Wenzel; Geraldyne Witkin; Steve Zientek.

The following business owners were very helpful: Elizabeth Cilker Smith (Cornerstone); Paul Dorsa (Opera House); Sue Farwell; Dave Flick; Teri Hope (Coffee Roasting Company); Carole Kattengrell (Twig); Ray Montalvo (Le Boulanger); Sarah Bayne, Head of Hillbrook School, and Ann Morrissey; Dennis Skaggs (Los Gatos Theater); and Pam Bancroft (The Terraces). Thanks to John Pugh and Eric Ziemelis for creating their public art and for allowing its inclusion here, and thanks to Amy Konsterlie for her watercolors of the town.

Thanks to the wonderful staff of the Los Gatos Public Library, especially Gloria Grimes. Thanks to the following architects and designers: Maurice Camargo; John Lien; Michael McKay; John Miller; Elle d'Lin; Gary Schloh; Chris Spaulding; Richard Stowers; Krista Wendt, Valerie Irene Zacher. Thanks to town officials and employees. The list would be exhaustive if I had asked everyone for help, but those I did ask were unstinting: Sandy Baily; Mardi Gualtieri Bennett; Lee Bowman; Cathleen Bruhn Boyer; Marian Cosgrove; Regina Falkner; Jan Hutchins; Tara Lang; MarLyn Rasmussen.

The following individuals provided information and insight that I sincerely appreciate: Sharon Anderegg; John Baggerly; Art Bonner; Bill Cotton; Teresa Crider; Pete Denevi; Paul Dubois; Pat Dunning; Mildred Garth; Helen Gillespie; Michael A. Green (grandson of George Green); Dr. & Mrs. Gregory Jenkins; Ralph Klindt; Father Tom Marshall, S. J.; Bill Quigley; Elayne Shuman; Peggy Stephenson (La Rinconada); Wilma Thompson; Lucy Wedemeyer; Kay Ytterboe. Special thanks to Ernest Patterson for providing the best story leads. And for encouragement and practical advice, thanks to Bille Jensen, author of *A Trip Through Time in the Santa Cruz Mountains*; Joshua Weisberg, color expert and technical wizard; and my undying gratitude to Richard Beal, author of *Highway 17*, for helping me overcome the last obstacle to making this book a reality.

Finally, I ask for your help in making this book more accurate. Please send any comments or corrections to my attention at Infospect Press.

Alastair Dallas (adallas@infospect.com)
Infospect Press
17681 Foster Road
Los Gatos, California 95030-7154

Introduction

By Kathryn Morgan

What Los Gatos and this book are not

Los Gatos has not been the scene of great wars or other historic events. It is not the site of architectural monuments like the Eiffel Tower, Leaning Tower, or Tower (shudder!) of London. Indeed, many of its adolescent inhabitants will loudly whine to you about what a boring place it is, with no action or excitement whatsoever. While a few murders have taken place in Los Gatos (including a rumored hanging from Main Street Bridge in the town's early days), and theft is all too common, most of the entries in the "Police Report" section of the local newspaper read something like: "On the day of the summer solstice a passer by reported a man under a tree in Oak Meadow Park chanting. He was counseled by police and sent on his way." Buying veggies at the Farmer's Market; watching little Indian Princesses and their dads, feathers waving, march in the Christmas Parade; pigging out on strawberries during June's Ming Quong (which means "Radiant Light" in Chinese-isn't that cool? Wasn't that a *bright* idea? Ha. You are lucky that Alastair and Mary asked me to write this introduction because I will regale you with tasty tidbits and (half-)witty puns. However I digress.) Strawberry Festival; attending a Town Council meeting to rant and rave at the defenseless and attentive and patient Town Council; touring historic homes; making a decision about which good restaurant to eat and drink at tonight; strolling or cruising North Santa Cruz Avenue—these are our ideas of big local action.

What this book and Los Gatos are

But Los Gatos has other, gentler, lovelier virtues. It is a fascinating microcosm of Western American small town history and architecture. Its local government, participated in by an inexhaustible pool of incredibly diverse, caring, broadminded, opinionated, and intelligent citizens, is one of the last bastions of participatory small town democracy. Its newspaper contains no

> ...inhabitants, past and present, are full of civic mindedness, vociferous opinions, education, achievements, eccentricities, and character. Most people love to visit here.

North Santa Cruz commercial

malicious gossip, does not violate citizen's privacy, and staffs no nosey papparazzi; instead it contains articles about real local issues and interesting local people; public-spirited, rational editorials; a "gossip" column publicizing citizen's good works and achievements; and letters to the editor and opinion pieces, some of them a little catty, by local contributors. Los Gatos' downtown and neighborhoods are beautiful, safe, walkable, friendly, and have great houses, landscaping, and flowers. Architecture ranges from the 1880 annex of our first building, Forbes Mill, through a few homes from the 1860s, a beautifully-preserved mix of Victorians and Craftsman bungalows, some delightful Art Deco from early in the 20th century, post-war tract houses, and sleek commercial buildings from recent decades. Its inhabitants, past and present, are full of civic mindedness, vociferous opinions, education, achievements, eccentricities, and character. Most people love to visit here.

It is these small town attributes that this beautifully written, helpfully organized, vividly illustrated and map-filled book will help you explore in Our Town, Los Gatos. Enjoy.

Where this book can lead you

If this book and walking around Los Gatos pique your interest, there are many other pathways to explore. Come visit our local Forbes Mill and Tait Avenue Museums (directions inside). Poke around down in the basement reference section of the Los Gatos Memorial Library. There you will find shelves of local history books behind the desk of the friendly reference librarian and local historic photographs on the walls around the bookstacks. Peruse the Santa Clara Library's well-organized archives of the Santa Clara Valley Historical and Genealogical Society. See what the Santa Clara County Recorder, Tax Assessor, and Surveyor's records can reveal. Gaze at historic Sanborn maps. Pursue the excellent bibliography at the end of this book. Talk or write to a local historian. (We're lousy with them, luckily for us.) How about investigating the history of the town where you yourself were born or raised, especially if you have relatives living there or ancestors resting there? You could research the architecture and history of your own home or your family's ancestral home.

Who knows what you will find? History, even of small towns, reveals insights, tragedies, hilarities and surprises—and some pretty juicy scandals, too, but that's another story. Call me up and I'll reveal some to you. Or e-mail me at kmorgan@lghs.net.

I hope you'll love this book as I have. I hope they'll give me a free copy for writing this introduction. I cannot wait to grab some unsuspecting guests and embark on the walking tours. Please do the same, and give the book as a souvenir to friends or family who stay here. Enough! Read on!

Kathryn Morgan

Kathryn Morgan has taught English at Los Gatos High School since 1966. She has served on the Los Gatos Planning Commission since 1982, she was a founding member of the Los Gatos Historic Preservation Committee and she chaired the first Citizen Task Force to revise the Town's General Plan in the early 1980s.

In 1987, Kathryn researched, wrote and directed the Los Gatos Centennial Pageant, a revival of a traditional outdoor spectacle. It was performed on the front lawn of the High School on August 8, 1987, the one hundredth anniversary of the town's incorporation. She looks forward to retirement, writing fiction, historic research and writing, more travelling to architectural and historic wonders throughout the world, becoming a Town Character, and perhaps playing Mrs. Santa Claus in the Los Gatos Christmas Parade.

Foreword

By Mary Tomasi-Dubois

As an impressionable teen in the early 60s, I was disappointed when I learned that my father had been transferred to Northern California. Having lived in the L. A. basin, close to Hollywood, I thought that Southern California was the only place to be. And to think of leaving an area where one could easily run into a matinee idol or starlet at the local market (never mind that I never had) crushed my young heart.

After having arrived in the Bay Area, I was discouraged in spite of the beauty all around me—orchard after orchard, beautiful hillsides, green everywhere, and no freeways! But it wasn't sophisticated Los Angeles with its bright lights and hustle and bustle, ever attractive to the young.

I quelled my aching by telling myself I was to live only an hour away from San Francisco with its hip coffeehouses, beat generation, intellectuals, and sophisticates. Then one sunny afternoon, my father took the family to lunch in a little hamlet called Los Gatos. That was it, my mood changed immediately. As any dramatic young girl might do, I decided that I would someday move to Los Gatos, and live the life of the "town and country" set, wearing a suede jacket, khaki slacks and loafers while driving my wood-paneled station wagon to the local market (I guess I hadn't left Hollywood completely behind). I would drive myself to the town every chance I got—for ice cream, the movies, and of course, pizza.

My schooling in architecture and architectural history helped pique my interest in the diverse Victorian, bungalow-style, and European-inspired buildings and homes of Los Gatos. When I discovered that there had been many famous personages who were living or had lived here, I forgot about Hollywood and even San Francisco. Los Gatos had its own sophistication and "hipness"—it would be cool to live here.

> My schooling in architecture and architectural history helped pique my interest in the diverse Victorian, bungalow-style, and European-inspired buildings and homes of Los Gatos.

Modern castle at 17461 High Street

ix

Well, that early dream came true (being part of the gentry and all). I've been in love with the town since the first day I saw it. Nestled at the base of the Santa Cruz Mountains, with its quaint "downtown," the charming neighborhoods, and practically everyone knowing everyone else gave me a sense of home. Sometimes I wear my khakis and loafers. But I drive my convertible to the farmer's market on warm Sunday mornings, have breakfast on Main Street, and enjoy working at Music In The Plaza in the late afternoon.

As an adult, I've become involved with many town organizations. Over coffee after working on a particular Kiwanis project, Alastair and I began talking about the interesting and diverse architecture here, as well as the famous architects who have lent their talents to help create the town's ambiance. I mentioned that, as part of the Arts Commission, I had joined a group discussion about putting together a booklet with information about various buildings, their architectural style, who might have lived in them, etc. to be used as a 'walking-tour' guide.

I could see Alastair's eyes light up. With his background and interest in architecture, he was ready to get started right away.

And, of course, he did–and in a big way! His efforts far exceeded what I had ever imagined. He's insightful, witty, knowledgeable, and erudite. His was a labor of love. The book recounts the history of Santa Clara County in general and Los Gatos in particular. But this is more than a history book. The reader can skip the front section and go directly to the guide (with clear maps included), savoring the history section over a steaming cup of cappuccino at a local coffee shop. I found the Origins of Place Names section of the Appendices to be especially interesting.

Not only can the book be used as a walking tour guide, but also, I think, will make a beautiful coffee table/library addition or a gift or memen-

to of one's visit to our beautiful town. It is very comprehensive, and the beautiful color photographs by photographer Peter Conrad help set the book apart from those that have proceeded it.

I am very pleased to have played a part in its production, and invite the reader to enjoy the journey on which he or she is about to embark.

Mary Tomasi-Dubois

Mary Tomasi-Dubois studied architecture in college, later changing her major to business. Today, she and her husband, Paul A. Dubois, own a security consulting and engineering firm here and live in town, as well. In addition to being co-owner, Mary provides space-planning services to their varied clientele. She also teaches basic architectural drafting to students pursuing their interior design associates certificate from U.C. Santa Cruz extension. She holds associate memberships with the American Society for Interior Design (ASID), the International Interior Design Association (IIDA), and the International Facility Managers Association (IFMA).

Mary currently chairs the Los Gatos Arts Commission, which is responsible for public art at the civic center and elsewhere and for the Music in the Plaza *series. Her husband, Paul, chairs the Community Services Commission, and both are active members of the Los Gatos Community Foundation and the local Kiwanis club.*

To Lee Bowman,

Town of Los Gatos Director of Planning
from 1973 to 1999.

Many of us only know him
through the beautiful town he
has guided to creation and
steadfastly helped to preserve.

His invisible hand and
patient vision have not
eliminated controversy, nor
is the town more than a
work in progress, but the
Los Gatos this book
observes owes much to
Lee Bowman.

MT. UMUNHUM, as serene as Japan's Mt. Fuji, rises 3,486 feet (1 km) above sea level, just southeast of Los Gatos. View toward Blossom Hill also shows Vasona Lake.

1 Gem of the Foothills

Los Gatos is a unique combination of old and new. A suburb of California's oldest and third largest city, San Jose, the Town of Los Gatos is a living museum of Victorian-era buildings and a vibrant tribute to the upscale values of its Silicon Valley residents. A university town lacking only the university, Los Gatos is an extraordinary yet ordinary place. While it shares features with a spectrum of cities from Palo Alto to Santa Cruz, Los Gatos is more intimate and more knowable. The ingredients may not be unique to Los Gatos, but the setting, events, and characters that created what we see today are not reproducible. There will never be another Los Gatos and its citizens, Los Gatans, cherish their town.

Living in town is expensive, in part because the public school district is excellent, but largely because of its proximity to the booming high technology industry in nearby Silicon Valley. Many of the people enjoying the town are visitors from near and far. Santa Clara County's Los Gatos Creek trail system cuts through town with convenient access to shopping and coffee. On summer and weekend nights, the sidewalks are packed with strolling people, here for the ambience of a fine restaurant or a self-guided gallery tour. During the winter holiday season, the trees are decorated, the sidewalks are packed with shoppers and horse-drawn carriages mingle with traffic.

> This other Eden, demi-paradise
>
> This fortress built by Nature for herself...
>
> This happy breed of men, this little world
>
> This precious stone...

PERHAPS SHAKESPEARE was in the minds of the boosters who named Los Gatos the "Gem of the Foothills."

THE PLACE TO BE: North Santa Cruz Avenue.

THE A. C. VOTE farm house, north of the town's original boundary, in the nearly forgotten district of Vineland (see 145).

WHAT MAKES LOS GATOS SPECIAL? The pleasant feelings that a stroll through Los Gatos elicits are, of course, complex, but they derive from at least five identifiable sources. First is the unusual architecture. The town's texture is intricate and multi-faceted, with a wide variety of spaces and vistas, rhythms, patterns, materials and colors. Second, the town encapsulates many reminders of the past, some subtle and others overt history. Third, the town is defined by the events, major and minor, which occur here on a regular basis—our traditions. Fourth, geography—the hills and the creek, in relation to the bay, the ocean and the equator, create an unequaled paradise. And, finally, Los Gatos is defined by her citizens and their community.

Architecture

The architecture of Los Gatos is eclectic. Much of the town's current charm derives from a blend of Victorian and Craftsman styles. One story cottages and bungalows sit side by side with two and two-and-a-half-story mansions adorned by large porches and self-confident turrets and cupolas. Other aspects of the town reflect the characteristics of these styles as well, reinforcing the values of integrity, care, balance, optimism and whimsy.

The earliest surviving buildings are straightforward American pioneer vernacular built from the two local materials: stone from the creek and redwood, which once thrived in the hills above town. As the town grew, Italianate and, later, Queen Anne Victorian buildings fronted on the dirt streets. Queen Anne style, in particular, expresses a picturesque, exuberant dynamism, with asymmetric towers and porches, windows that pop out, straining to be nearer to the street, meticulous decoration on many surfaces and crowning every fold, unconventional color, tasteful variety, and modest puffery.

The Arts and Crafts movement found resonance in Los Gatos as the town matured, and many beautiful Craftsman homes and bungalows remain. The Craftsman ethic represents a more serious side of the town's character, with its emphasis on natural, hand-worked materials and undisguised constructions. The town's inventory of early twentieth-century buildings also includes a cornucopia of Pennsylvania Dutch gambrels, one or two Colonial mansions, the Greek Revival high school, and a few unique structures that resolutely defy labeling. The more recent architecture has had fewer unqualified successes, but the town is demonstrably not living in its past, as witness the timeless, self-effacing Civic Center, built in 1965.

A few famous architects have worked in Los Gatos, names such as Polk, Maybeck, Morgan and, recently, Saitowitz and Turnbull. Willis Jefferson Polk of San Francisco, a brash young man with diverse stylistic influences, is credited with launching the California Mission Revival movement in the 1890s. Polk directed the renovation of the McCullagh estate, *La Estancia*. His contemporary, Bernard Maybeck of Berkeley, is one father of the Craftsman bungalow. (Maybeck's work in Los Gatos is, unfortunately, not completely documented.) Julia Morgan, famous as the designer of Hearst Castle at San Simeon, built the Clara Huntington Perkins House above Fairview in 1919-1920. Modern architects, such as South African Stanley Saitowitz and the late William Turnbull, Jr., designer of the seminal Sea Ranch project, have also built works in town.

COFFEE, ART, AND A SALOON upstairs called Mountain Charley's.

The design of Los Gatos as a whole exhibits the desirable traits of propinquity, pedestrian scale and serendipity. Everything in this town seems close at hand: one shop is next to another, and the string of village-scaled parking lots is adjacent to the shops and restaurants. Many residents routinely walk to town, and apartments here and there are tucked in above the stores.

These adjacencies make Los Gatos a walking town, a pedestrian experience, and the rich detail of the buildings and appurtenances reflects the fact. Elsewhere, regional shopping malls may have walls that are sheer planes stretching thirty or forty feet in the air—such architecture is designed to be experienced at freeway speed. In contrast, Los Gatos' variety at eye-level and the human scale of its doors, windows, passages and spaces make it a pleasant place to be outside one's automobile. The town is not boring.

WILLIAM TURNBULL, JR., of Sea Ranch fame, designed the Melinda Stewart House (see 131).

Propinquity can also mean juxtaposition, the setting of one experience against the backdrop of something much different. Los Gatos creates this effect so often that the thoughtful observer has moments of frisson, of seeing things from another perspective. Architects who follow Charles Moore call this heightened and unexpected perception serendipity. (Moore defines other terms, as well, including inhabitation, "the human act of being...in a space ennobled by our presence...a powerful reality that architecture is supposed to be all about but more often isn't.")

La Cañada building at sunset.

LIKE A MACHINE-TOOLED EGGPLANT, a 1937 Cord helps illustrate the timeless sophistication of today's Glen Ridge Park.

These esoteric observations add up to something more tangible—they're good for business. The pedestrian environment is less rushed, and the profuse variety of spatial and design experiences promotes feelings of well being. While clearly beneficial to residents and attractive to visitors, this is precisely the mood that merchants want customers in as well.

Shopping downtown, leaving the car and strolling the sidewalks window-shopping, is a signature activity in Los Gatos, and the design qualities of propinquity, taste, and style extend to much of the merchandise. Shaved chocolate on the flourish of whipped cream at the bakery or the coffee house, an elegant velvet backdrop for a glittering diamond, the perfect frame on a piece of art that seizes your senses and won't let go. The camera pulls back and the setting is an artful, trendy shop interior. The exterior is a restored Victorian on a vibrant sidewalk a short walk from a true neighborhood filled with antique cottages behind white picket fences. As the camera zooms out, the town is visibly nestled in the folds of the hills near the center of the 21st century information economy.

History

Los Gatos is appreciated as a living museum, an idealized yet functional Main Street, U. S. A. It is Our Town, decorated with banners, substantial banks, and an All-American high school with cheerleaders and the Wildcats football squad. It is "morning in America," and It's a Wonderful Life.

The past, particularly buildings and trees, if not cultures and lifestyles, is preserved here by law. Buildings built before 1940 may not be altered without special permission; many are designated for historical recognition and a half dozen are listed with the National Historic Register. Some sparse settlement in this area occurred in the 1830s, but the majority of the old buildings date to around the time of the town's incorporation in 1887. Buildings from the 1860s and 1870s are few and they are hard to date precisely. Although Forbes Mill was built in 1854, all that remains of it is an annex built in 1880. The original adobes are gone and the first American house, near the Mill, along with the original waystation called the Ten Mile House, are all destroyed. The town has taken steps to preserve the remaining buildings, including a comprehensive historic resources inventory commis-

sioned following the October 1989 earthquake. In 1976, the Bellringer project (and Bellringer II in 1986) recognized and rewarded citizens who restored their classic homes.

Los Gatos also treasures its trees. Native Coast Live Oak and imported Eucalyptus trees dominate, but Deodar Cedar, Washingtonian Palm, and many other varieties are everywhere. And once here, they may not be removed (or in some cases even trimmed) without due process. This policy has created an arboreal canopy over much of the town, eliminating the sweeping vistas captured in antique photos.

Traditions

Places are defined by things that happen in them regularly. One signature activity in Los Gatos is meeting friends for a cup of coffee after, perhaps, a bike ride on the creek trail. Saturday mornings find dozens of spandex-clad joggers and bicyclists enjoying the fresh air and sipping fresh-brewed coffee. Others wait, visiting with friends and neighbors, for a seat at one of several downtown breakfast restaurants. After sunset, as urbane couples stroll past the galleries, teenagers haunt North Santa Cruz Avenue to see and be seen. And the pubs, from C. B. Hannegan's to the Los Gatos Brewing Company, the Black Watch to the Los Gatos Bar & Grill, or the Last Call, are always crowded.

Other moments which recur are less obvious. Seven o'clock on Sunday morning will find many Los Gatans tending their gardens and others sipping tea on the porch. Meetings of the town council are held in the evening when citizens can attend, and they do. The five council members are listed in the phone book. An observer's tour of the town will surely yield potential car purchasers—especially young people—ogling Ferraris while their

WEST MAIN STREET (bridge at far right) in 1883. Almost none of these buildings survive, with the exception of the white building near the center—St. Mary's, which was moved. The open space immediately beyond St. Mary's is the so-called Almond Grove and the gentle brow to its left is Glen Ridge.

FOURTH OF JULY concert on the High School lawn.

5

WILDCATS OF LOS GATOS High School emblem features the orange and black school colors.

SYMBOLS OF THE TOWN, these concrete cats guard the entrance to Poet's Canyon (see 123).

GARY EHLERT, town commissioner and resident of Broadway, has led the Holiday Parade for nearly ten years with his 1955 T-bird, believed to be the first Thunderbird delivered to Santa Clara County.

dates feign interest. Renovation and building are a constant. Dumpsters and contractors' pickup trucks dot the residential streets. Weddings and other events at the History Club or the Opera House make limousines a familiar sight as well. Los Gatos has fifteen parks, and grownups support the children in organized sports like Little League and Soccer. The World Cup champion Brazilian soccer team had people dancing in the streets here a few years ago. And Los Gatos High School takes its football very seriously—former coach Charlie Wedemeyer was the subject of *Quiet Victory*, a 1988 made-for-television movie staring Michael Nouri.

Speaking of celebrities, Los Gatos is home to a few, including Olympic gold medallist Peggy Fleming and one of the inventors of the personal computer, philanthropist Steve Wozniak. The town has attracted famous visitors since its inception. The list includes President Benjamin Harrison in the 1890s and President Bill Clinton and Vice-President Al Gore in the 1990s. Henry Kissinger lived on Massol Avenue and helped form the first service club, the Kiwanis, in 1923…but he was not related to the future Secretary of State. Allan and Malcolm Loughhead lived in the hills south of town in 1913 when they flew the first plane over San Francisco Bay—their company became known as Lockheed. Henry Ford and Thomas Edison spent a day and a night in Los Gatos in 1915. Jack London's first wife and children lived on Broadway. Family and friends of celebrities have occasioned regular visits from George Burns and his wife Gracie Allen, former president Herbert Hoover, and Sarah Winchester, builder of the Mystery House. Jack Kerouac and other "beat generation" celebrities visited Neal Cassady in the 1960s. Location filming brought Orson Welles here in 1970 and Dustin Hoffman was seen dining in Los Gatos in 1997 while shooting *Mad City* in San Jose. There is also a rumor that Joe DiMaggio and his bride Marilyn Monroe spent the first night of their honeymoon here in 1954. Dave Goelz, one of the Muppets (Gonzo the Great to be precise), lived on Fairview Plaza before stardom. Gary Dahl invented the Pet Rock here in 1976. And actor Vincent Price was known to "haunt" our antique stores in the early 1970s.

Los Gatos has a reputation as an artist colony, as well. Violinist Lord Yehudi Menuhin, perhaps one of the Doobie Brothers, actress Olivia de Havilland and her sister Joan Fontaine, writer

6

John Steinbeck, and poets Ruth Comfort Mitchell, Sara Bard Field, and Henry Meade Bland have lived here. Contemporary artists Bruni and John Pugh are Los Gatans. The children of Los Gatos, some of them perhaps future artists, recently decorated the Forbes Mill footbridge with over 36 unique murals.

Every Sunday morning, an open-air street market closes Montebello Way. Throughout the summer, Music in the Plaza offers free concerts on Sunday afternoons. Each August, the *Fiesta de Artes* art and wine festival, sponsored by the local Kiwanis club, occupies the civic center. Early in December the festive season is heralded by the Tree Lighting ceremony, followed the next day by the home-spun Children's Holiday Parade, featuring hundreds of marchers (many of them children) and thousands of spectators, often televised on San Jose television. Another holiday tradition is the lovely sound of horse-drawn carriages making their way through downtown traffic.

Every day of the year, Los Gatos is a delight to the senses. The aromas downtown range from those that emanate from several bakeries to fresh-brewed coffee to candy to wood-fired pizza. There is the yeasty smell from the vats at the Brewing Company, or the pungent aroma from the town's cigar lounges. Alpine Avenue and other streets are rich with the scent of pine, while towering, fragrant eucalyptus line streets like Overlook and Hilow Road.

Roosters crow with the dawn in some parts of town, and donkeys, including the pair at the Novitiate named Jack and Jill, snort and bray at visitors. The near-silent hum of passing bicycles on the creek trail blends with the squeals of delighted children at the town's playgrounds, and the relaxing gurgle of moving water soothes the ear at the civic center and the town plaza. Los Gatos is a sensual town, from the dappled sunlight under the trees at the tiny Fairview Park to the shiny, curvaceous automobiles, and from the broad spectrum of art and antiques to the public art of John Pugh's trompe l'oeils or civic center sculpture.

THE CHILDREN'S HOLIDAY PARADE is overseen by the cameras of KICU-TV, San Jose, as well as the by the venerable turret of the La Canada Block (see 7).

LOS GATOS HIGH SCHOOL. Watercolor by Amy Konsterlie.

Los Gatos Creek Trail

Ignorance killed the cat, sir. Curiosity was framed...

Geography

The Gem City of the Foothills enjoys a lovely setting. The climate is perfect for growing most fruits and nuts, with a short winter rainy season and extremely rare snowfall. Los Gatos is 37 degrees above the equator, like Richmond, Virginia, Tokyo, Japan and the Mediterranean Sea. The town is just 300 feet (92 m) above sea level, with a 3,200 foot (975 m) mountain backdrop, the Sierra Azul, shielding it from the coastal fog of Santa Cruz. Mt. Umunhum (*yoo' mê num*), to the east, rises 3,486 feet (1063 m) above San Francisco Bay.

The fruitful Santa Clara Valley was originally known as the "Valley of Heart's Delight." The soil of Los Gatos has grown countless prunes, apricots, apples, and grapes, and although only one or two orchards remain, new vineyards are being planted.

Community

Los Gatans love their town. The real estate term "pride of ownership" applies to just about every house in town. There is a weekly newspaper, but concerned neighbors keep each other informed and attend council meetings in large numbers when the issues demand. The town council recently empanelled a grassroots citizens' Task Force to plan for growth over the next twenty years.

There are churches (and thriving congregations) of most every denomination here. The Methodist church, at 132 years old, was first; it was followed by the Presbyterian church; St. Luke's Episcopal Church; St. Mary's Catholic Church, and many others.

And the town is served by several strong service clubs and fraternal orders, including Kiwanis (the first), Rotary, Lions, Optimists, Elks, and the Masons.

There were 30,100 residents in Los Gatos at last count. The average age is 39, there are more women (52.2%) than men, and more than half are currently married. A slight majority are registered Republican, but nearly one-fifth of the registered voters belong to an independent party or are just plain independent.

In the early 1960s, 99.2% of the town was Caucasian, while the 1990 census showed that figure declining, with 97.8% of residents being either white or Asian. (Santa Clara County as a whole is 30% non-white.)

Los Gatos is also unusual in its growth trends. A recent study by the Association of Bay Area Governments predicted that by 2015, San Jose's population would increase by 18%, and that Morgan Hill would grow by 53%. The same study expected Los Gatos to grow by just 2%, or fewer than 600 new residents.

Los Gatos Theater, 41 N. Santa Cruz Ave. (see 10).

There is no denying that Los Gatos is upscale, with its Ferrari dealer, art galleries, haute cuisine, athletic clubs, micro-brewery, and bocce ball. Simple cottages have become mansions thanks to a booming real estate market. The town has many unique galleries and antique stores as well as high-end chains such as Starbucks, Borders, Oakville Grocery, and the Chart House restaurant. The latest trends, such as fine cigar shops and clubs are also showing up here. Personalized license plates adorn expensive cars whose drivers seem perpetually distracted by their portable phones. Petite housewives pilot huge sport-utility vehicles into and out of "compact" parking spaces.

Jewelry on North Santa Cruz Avenue.

Yet the town is not elitist or exclusionary. The new arrivals co-exist with people who grew up here. A large elderly constituency live in town, many in facilities like The Meadows or The Terraces, and the town is well served by the county-wide Valley Transit Authority. Low-income housing is sprinkled through town, including apartments above some newer buildings downtown, and the busy Community Services department helps a wide variety of charities.

The town's embarrassment of riches makes its preservation of the past and its serene ambience possible. The Victorian houses were once considered just old, too expensive to take care of. Thanks to the tilted economics, people can afford to lovingly restore their home's meticulous gingerbread, and collectors can grace the avenues with their mint-condition automobiles. There are many opinions among Los Gatos residents, but one goal seems common to all—to preserve the unique small-town character, the special ambience, of Los Gatos.

MEN AT WORK at Forbes Mill, circa 1900. Two-story annex (built 1880) behind the wooden bridge is all that remains of the 1854 structure.

2 Perspective

Los Gatos began as a stop on the road from San Jose to Santa Cruz which served the needs of mountain lumbermen. But as the redwood forests were depleted and the railroad arrived, fruit and tourism became important and Los Gatos came into its own. A thriving town emerged in the 1880-1915 period, and many of the Victorian and Craftsman buildings from that era remain. During the 1950s, the freeway brought a different kind of progress to the town and for a time it seemed that only new things received the proper attention. More recently the town has come to respect both old and new.

Rancho Rinconada de Los Gatos

Although the El Camino Real between Mission Santa Cruz and Mission Santa Clara ran through Los Gatos as early as 1791, this area was largely uninhabited—with the exception of the nomadic Coastanoan, or Ohlone Indians—until the 1840s. California had been colonized by the Catholic church, but the mission system broke down fol-

1791

lowing the Mexican Revolution in 1821. For the next two decades, the governor of Alta California encouraged settlement by granting land to those who would establish the grant's boundaries and agree to build and occupy a house on the land. After years of petitioning, José Maria Hernandez and his brother-in-law Sebastian Fabian Peralta were granted one and a half leagues (6,631.44 acres) in the south-west corner of the Santa Clara Valley on July 23, 1839. Because neither could read nor write, they each signed for their land with an 'X'.

1839

The origins of the name Los Gatos are in some dispute, but town historian William Wulf argues that the ridgeline between the town and Mission Santa Cruz had long been called cuesta de los gatos, or ridge of the cats, referring to the wild cats often seen in the hills. In 1978, Wulf persuaded the United States Geological Survey to officially restore the ridge's original name. The creek which flowed from the ridge was traditionally called Los Gatos Creek (although it has had

Ohlone Village (Vanessa Pinheiro)

several names), and Hernandez and Peralta named their grant *La Rinconada de los Gatos*—the corner of the cats. As required by the terms of the grant, they each built a house along the creek: Hernandez in what is now Vasona Park and Peralta near the border with Campbell. Both houses were built of bricks made from dried creek mud, or adobe, and unfortunately, both of these original buildings are long gone.

The man who built the first commercial building in the area, and thus is credited with founding the town, was born in Scotland in 1805, educated by Jesuits in Argentina and Montevideo, Uruguay, and fought as a privateer against Argentina's claims on Uruguay before arriving in California in October 1831. In 1842, having married Anna Maria Galindo, the daughter of the major domo of the Mission Santa Clara, James Alexander Forbes was serving at least two masters. He was the British vice consul, one of the agents who might help the crown seize Northern California (at least) from Mexico, in order to extend Britain's Oregon Territory claims southward. At the same time, his father-in-law, the major domo, asked him to oversee the mission's share of a mercury mine in the hills east of what would become Los Gatos.

War with Mexico

War between the United States and Mexico over Texas and California territories seemed likely in the 1840s, but whether the British might act belligerently was not clear. California's true worth, particularly her mineral resources, was not yet known. Quicksilver, or mercury, is a vital ingredient in extracting gold and silver ore, and the mines at Almaden, Spain held a lucrative near-monopoly on the unique liquid metal. The discovery of mercury on the Capitancillos Rancho was thus nearly as important as gold. The mine—which would eventually prove richer than the great quicksilver mine in Spain—was named Nuevo Almaden. It was owned by a group of Mexican investors and the Mission Santa Clara.

Alexander Forbes, of the far-flung British trading company Barron & Forbes' office in Tepíc, Mexico, learned of the quicksilver discovery and

David Hembry's painting illustrates the story of Yoscolo, a native Californian who led 200 of his people from the Mission Santa Clara in 1831. They were captured near Los Gatos and their leader's head was mounted on a spike outside the mission.

James Forbes (Katherine Pease)

the firm quickly bought up shares in the New Almaden mine, though the Mission Santa Clara's shares were not for sale. Alexander Forbes was James' uncle (although some accounts dispute this) and, like his nephew, was also working for British interests. The British had helped finance Mexico's revolution against Spain in 1821 and Barron & Forbes' shipments of gold via San Francisco were in repayment of this debt. That is, Barron & Forbes had a legal basis for effectively smuggling Mexican gold. Whether the final accounting added up or not is subject to speculation. (Mexican soldiers were looking for Alexander Forbes when he hastily left the country in the mid-1850s.) The money to build a mill that would establish Los Gatos may have been a "handling fee" charged by the local vice consul.

Barron & Forbes took action to increase production at the Quicksilver mine, and the sheriff was involved with a dispute between James and Barron & Forbes' emissary, Robert Walkinshaw. After helping to establish the British mine, James turned his attention to building a British mill.

There were as many intrigues as there were interests in California in the years before the Gold Rush, and both Barron & Forbes and the Major

Domo's son-in-law were probably trying to secure these resources for Great Britain. Meanwhile, each agent was probably looking, quite naturally, after his own fortune. Opportunity was everywhere. The only thing certain about the political situation was that Mexico was probably too weak to retain Alta California. It would become a province of Britain, Russia or the United States.

Communication with headquarters was the main problem for Britain's agents and the other players as well. The attempt to secure California's mineral resources for Great Britain failed when other events overtook it. In early 1846, John C. Frémont raised an army of Americans living in California against Mexico. Traveling around the state, he and his men camped near today's Santa Theresa in February and detoured through the foothills on their way to Santa Cruz rather than confront Los Gatos ranchero Sebastian Peralta, who accused the "army" of stealing his horses. They camped at the summit on February 22. By June, independence-minded Californians were calling for the establishment of a "Bear Flag Republic" that would probably have fallen to one of the larger powers in any event. On May 13, 1846, the United States had declared war on Mexico, and Commodore Sloat occupied Monterey harbor for the U. S. Navy in July. Neither Sloat nor Frémont had specific orders to claim California, but neither wanted the other to beat him to it. Sloat acted first, ending the English claim on the New Almaden Mine and on California, because Britain sought de facto control, not outright war.

1846

Forty-niners crossing the plains (Ryan Burrow)

The Gold Rush and Statehood

While this low-intensity war waged on, thirteen survivors of the Donner Party settled in San José, including one Isaac Branham (1803-c1882), member of a group that crossed the Sierra by a different route in October 1846.

Branham, and a sea captain named Julian Hanks, bought a steam engine shipped around Cape Horn and built the first sawmill in this county on November 29, 1847 where Lexington Reservoir is today, and established a lumber yard just east of today's Main Street bridge. In January, 1848, gold was discovered at Sutter's Mill near Sacramento, and in February, the Treaty of Guadalupe Hidalgo made California officially United States territory. Meeting in Monterey in September 1849, delegates, including Julian Hanks, established the first California State government.

1847

Although several grist mills had been built in the county, the first in 1842, the gold rush created a huge demand for flour to feed the hungry forty-niners. Nearly the entire valley was growing wheat, but mill capacity was lacking. James Forbes purchased 2,000 acres from José Hernandez with promises in 1850 and began planning an ambitious, four-story stone flour mill on Los Gatos Creek. Construction of Forbes' Mill finally began October 1852 and took some two years, but the grand structure established the town of Los Gatos. Because the mail to Santa Cruz passed through this area, letters were dropped off as early as 1849, but mail was first officially delivered to the new town at the Mill in 1854. Forbes, overextended by his ambitious plans, and perhaps affected by Barron & Forbes' situation in Mexico, went bankrupt in December 1856. It is not clear whether Hernandez was ever paid a penny.

1849

Mountain Charlie by "LKR"

FORBES MILL became the Los Gatos Manufacturing Company in 1866 and many improvements were made, including extending the flume and installing a turbine in place of the original 20' (6m) diameter overshot wheels. A bridge from the third floor at the right of the photo connected the mill to the LG Mfg. Co. offices and general store on East Main.

While the gold rush raged in the Sierra Nevada, the Santa Cruz Mountains experienced a redwood rush. It is reported that redwood forests were visible from Los Gatos until they were brutally clear cut in the early days of the state. Zachariah "Buffalo" Jones and his wife Mary bought the Branham/Hanks mill for $3,000. Jones expanded the mill, located in what was known as "Cañon de Arroyo" (Creek Canyon) and renamed the creek, the canyon and everything in sight after himself. Jones Road, the steep, narrow trail from the mill down to Jones' lumber yard where the Penthouse Apartments stand today, still exists. Most of the route is now a public recreational trail. It is easy to stop at an isolated portion of the trail and imagine coaxing a horse-drawn wagon, filled with cut lumber, using ropes, chains and a special metal skid fitted under the wagon to slide over obstacles.

Santa Cruz Turnpike

To avoid Jones' property, the Santa Cruz Turnpike Company was formed in 1858. The county issued charters to encourage construction of public roads allowing a company to charge tolls for twenty years to recover costs, after which the road would be free for all. The new road cut the travel time to Santa Cruz to just a half day. Historian William Wulf has discovered that one of the first fares on the new road was a circus—he tells the colorful story of a line of elephants making their way through Mountain Charley's land at the summit, up and around switchbacks and finally down to Santa Cruz. Mountain Charley charged his own tolls, at times, but his house was refuge to many and the famed bear-fighter rescued more than one unwary traveler. After fighting the public road unsuccessfully in court, Buffalo Jones sold out to John P. Henning who renamed the settlement Lexington, after Lexington, Missouri, just east of Kansas City (and not, as some say, after Lexington, Kentucky).

1858

FORBES MILL on the bank of Los Gatos Creek
(Spencer Lopes)

Redwood Economy to Fruit Economy

As the Civil War began a continent away, pioneers were settling Los Gatos. John Lyndon of Vermont landed in San Francisco (by way of Panama) in October 1859 and found work in the mill at Lexington. He parlayed his savings into Willow Glen real estate and later made investments in Los Gatos. Peter Johnson arrived from Denmark in 1861. A teamster, he established a stable at Los Gatos to support the heavy wagon traffic bringing Santa Cruz lumber to the valley and ports like Redwood City. Lyman Burrell experimented with fruit trees in the Los

Gatos hills in the 1850s, just as the first local vineyards were planted. The first wooden house in town was built by a Mr. Samuels in 1861, at Main and Church. (The home was later purchased by W. S. McMurtry and survived until the 1950s.) Like Johnson, Henry D. McCobb, formerly Santa Clara's postmaster, invested in Los Gatos to take advantage of the heavy wagon traffic. In 1864, McCobb bought one hundred acres, including today's Broadway district, and became the proprietor of the one-room redwood cabin, constructed in 1860, on the site of today's Toll House. This cabin was the town's first hotel, built by a retired stagecoach driver named Rockyfellow. Because it was ten miles south of San Jose, it was known as the Ten Mile House. Also in 1864, John J. Roberts settled in today's Vasona Park and built a family farmhouse on the site of the Hernandez adobe, which had returned to mud during a particularly wet winter. The first post office was established at Los Gatos in the Ten Mile House on December 8, 1864.

California was fifteen years old and was still not linked to the east by rail. The Civil War was still raging, and Governor Leland Stanford and his friends were building the empire that would become the Southern Pacific railroad. In 1865,

A HORSE RACE, possibly Mt. Charley trailing Lyman Burrell. (Yvonne Lin)

SPIRIT OF THE BEAR by Stephanie Williams

the year President Lincoln was assassinated, James Kennedy built a house and a toll gate at the entrance to Los Gatos Canyon—the site gives the Toll House Hotel its name. When there was only one gate, in Lexington, the teamsters were charged the full toll whether or not they went to Santa Cruz. As grantors of the right to levy tolls, the county forced the Turnpike Company to install a gate at Los Gatos.

In 1866, Los Gatos really began to grow. W. H. Rogers had purchased Forbes Mill for $12,000 (it reportedly cost Forbes $80,000 to build), and Rogers & Co. installed a turbine and extended the flume in 1866, increasing the mill's power. In that same year, Thomas Shannon built a home in the foothills east of town, and the First Methodist Church was established. Donald Mackenzie, with his eye on Los Gatos Creek, formed the San Jose Water Company. By 1868, Los Gatos had a mill, a blacksmith, a stage depot, a lumberyard, a temporary schoolhouse, a hotel incorporating a post office, and several houses, and it was eclipsing Lexington in regional importance. After his hotel burned to the ground one Saturday night in 1868, Henry McCobb considered subdividing his acreage and renaming the town Cobbsville. Instead, he sold his 100 acre proper-

ty to John Weldon Lyndon for $7,500. Lyndon rebuilt the Ten Mile House, with two stories, south of today's post office.

In 1870, J. W. McMillan and Dr. W. S. McMurtry invested in Forbes Mill and moved to town. McMurtry became postmaster, and he and his partners extended the mill's flume for the second time, raising the head to two hundred feet (61 m), and also established a separate water-powered woolen mill next door. During the 1870s, John Lyndon speculated in Los Gatos and bought and sold the Ten Mile House at least twice. The transcontinental train arrived in California in 1869, after the driving of the golden spike, but tracks did not extend toward Los Gatos for another ten years. The railroad connecting Los Gatos with the world was the brainchild of James G. Fair, one of the instant millionaires created by the Comstock silver mines. With the Santa Cruz toll road's twenty year franchise due to expire and the train heading for town, angry teamsters tore down Mr. Kennedy's toll gates on November 15, 1877 and then dumped the replacement gate unceremoniously into Los Gatos Creek in January 1878. John Lyndon sold two parcels of land to give the railroad a north-south right-of-way and the deal provided that the railroad would pay to move the Ten Mile House across the street to the site of today's Lyndon Plaza. The first train on the South Pacific Coast line arrived from Newark on March 20, 1878. Work continued on the extension to Santa Cruz, which was completed over the next two years.

Railroad Transforms Town

1881

One day in May or June, 1881, William S. Walker, a farmer from Missouri who had made a name in printing and newspaper publishing in towns in Illinois, Missouri, Nebraska and California, stepped off the train in Los Gatos. He had decided to publish a newspaper in Saratoga, and this was as close as the train came. Leaving the Los Gatos Hotel across from the depot to more common visitors, Mr. Walker traveled the length of Main Street, crossing the creek on the aging bridge, to reach the Coleman House, the town's newest and possibly most elegant hostelry. The Coleman House stood on the north side of Main across from Alpine Avenue.

William Walker decided quickly that things were more likely to happen in Los Gatos than in Saratoga. The first issue of the Los Gatos *Weekly News* was published July 2, 1881 from a house on Alpine Avenue. Soon, Walker was meeting with important men in town like Samuel Templeton, Thomas Shannon, Herman Sund and Peter Johnson, discussing the construction of a cannery in town and wooden sidewalks for tourists.

A first class wooden bridge, high enough to withstand the annual floods, was built across the creek between the mill and the hotel in 1882, and it marked not just the town's "main street," but its coming of age. During the early 1880s, a

SUBSTANTIAL BRICK buildings with sophisticated urban ornamentation began to appear around the train depot in the early 1890s.

schoolhouse was built on University Avenue (the Old Town site), St. Mary's Catholic Church was built at Bean and Santa Cruz Avenue, and the Los Gatos Canning Company, managed by George Hooke, was built about where the Los Gatos Theater is today. John Lyndon expanded his hotel, and also invested in the Los Gatos Gas Company, the Los Gatos Bank, and in the Canning Company. (In 1889, Lyndon was the town's second-highest taxpayer, responsible for 5% of the town's revenue.) The town had seven saloons; Alexander Place's Furniture and Undertaking establishment on Main Street; a second newspaper, the *Mail*; an Opera House (Seanor's, near today's Masonic Lodge), and the Sunset Telephone Company. The redwood economy of Lexington had been replaced by a fruit economy centered in Los Gatos.

Herman Sund, a Swedish immigrant, emerged as the town's leading builder, and orchardist John Cilker established the Co-op Winery. Both left lasting legacies. Sund's original farmhouse remains, along with many of the buildings he and his son built (Russell Sund built the Tait Museum, and the Mail-News Building, to name two examples). The stone walls of the Co-op Winery still stand behind the civic center, and the Cilker family developed the Cornerstone retail center (at Blossom Hill Road and Los Gatos Boulevard) and donated some of the land on which Good Samaritan Hospital was built in the 1960s.

THE FIRE'S AFTERMATH of October 13, 1901. Viewpoint is toward the familiar La Cañada turret through the not-yet-existent Coffee Roasting Company, with the new Lyndon Hotel on the left.

As the town grew, little neighborhoods were carved from larger farms and orchards. John Lyndon subdivided the property between the hillside known as Los Gatos Meadow (now The Meadows retirement home) and his hotel (today's Lyndon Plaza) and grandly called the street leading straight to the railroad depot "Broadway." Peter Johnson subdivided his 131 acres and created Johnson Avenue and, somewhat hopefully, Market Street. Herman Sund established a lumber yard on Johnson, but commercial businesses tended to locate near the railroad, however, and the street was renamed Loma Alta many years after Johnson's death.

Hernandez and Peralta had divided their original 6,600-acre rancho three ways in the 1850s and Edward Auzerais of San Jose came to own the western-most third. John Mason purchased 162½ acres from Auzerais in 1865 and by 1880 had about 90 acres left. Benjamin Franklin Bachman, the never-married one-time postmaster of Mariposa (1862-65), bought 50 of these acres in 1880 on elevated land overlooking the Santa Cruz (or Lexington) Road and planted 500 French prune trees, 500 peaches, 400 apricots, 700 almonds and a smattering of cherries, pears and plums. Mason's remaining 40 acres were sold over the next few years to: an orchardist from Springfield, Ohio (originally from Michigan) named John Bean; a banker named Alphonse Eli Wilder; Augustine Nicholson, a "capitalist" (businessman); Fenilen "Fen" Massol; and a farmer, miner and Civil War veteran named Captain Magnus Tait. Tait was something of a celebrity, thanks to his book, *My Rebel Prison Life*, describing his travails as a Union prisoner of war.

This group conspired to create a subdivision known as the Almond Grove, with broad streets

Been There, Done That, Got the Doorbell

ABOUT ONE HUNDRED HOMES in Los Gatos proudly display the brass wildcat plaque shown here. What does it mean and how can you get one? Unfortunately, the plaques were always intended to be a limited edition in order not to diminish the prestige of the award.

Bellringer plaques were awarded to 62 homeowners on June 26, 1976 at a barbecue on the Los Gatos High School lawn as part of the town's celebration of the nation's bicentennial. Conceived by Mardi Gualtieri Bennett, the project was an adjunct of the Los Gatos Bicentennial Committee, and was headed by Ed Dowd, with architectural consultation from Dennis Burrow. Ms. Bennett was elected to the town council in 1976 and served as mayor 1978-79. She later wrote *Images of Long Ago*, a collection of vintage photographs and historical anecdotes about Los Gatos.

Only homes built before 1900 were eligible for the award, thus leaving out many fine Craftsman houses and much of Glen Ridge. Owners had to propose restoration work, have it approved and complete it before the award. This proved impractical, and the rules were later relaxed to allow qualifying refurbishment that had been completed since 1973.

The original Bellringer homes ranged from modest (64 Central) to grand (45 Broadway). Applications were carefully screened, because it appears that everyone who applied was accepted. Broadway had eight Bellringers, the most of any street, with Glenridge, Los Gatos Boulevard and University beating out Fairview Plaza, Edelen and Hernandez.

Six additional plaques were awarded July 4, 1977. Project Bellringer II was organized by Sara Anderson in 1984. This time the team included Mardi Bennett, historian William Wulf, architect Gary Schloh and Regina Falkner of the town's Community Services Department. Thirty-two homes were honored in January 1987 to celebrate the town's centennial, and this time Los Gatos Boulevard was the most represented, easily surpassing Tait and Wilder. The obviously historic homes of Peter Johnson, Daniel Simons and the Forrest family of Oak Meadow were among the honorees.

The original plaques were cast in brass by students at Los Gatos High School using funds donated by the Lions Club. Joe Mander designed them using Lynn Johnston's wildcat artwork.

but impossibly tiny lots compared to the farms and orchards of the area. Would anyone buy a 50-foot lot and build a home? Pooling their energy, they publicized their tract and special trains brought buyers from San Francisco on September 3, 1887 (the first month of the town's official existence). One hundred twenty-one lots were sold on the first day. Other early developers include John Miles and his friend Mr. Edelen, who made The Vineyard (now the Edelen district) available in the early 1880s.

The Town Incorporates

The one square mile Town of Los Gatos was officially incorporated August 10,

The Hotel Lyndon (Jamie M. Franks)

1887. Palmer C. Perkins, the first chairman of the Board of Trustees (that is, the mayor), sold "Stoves & Tinware" at 98 West Main (near today's Coffee Roasting Company). The Society of Jesus, having bought Harvey Wilcox's 39 acres just east of the creek the year before, began construction on a Novitiate, or Jesuit training school, that year. For the next sixty years, the Jesuits steadily expanded, continuing to press sacramental wine from Wilcox's vineyards even during Prohibition. By 1968, when the current building was constructed, the fathers owned over 400 acres of land, giving the town a backdrop of unspoiled hills.

John Bean's two sons-in-law, Dr. Robert Gober and David C. Crummey, commissioned C. F.

Scammon to build a mansion at the corner of Bean and Santa Cruz Avenue. Dr. Gober made house calls for the next fifty years. Bean and Crummey, seizing an opportunity, formed the Mountain Spring Water Company and constructed facilities in 1891-92. Their reservoir, bought by San Jose Water, still stands on Manzanita Avenue, and the pump house at the end of Bean Avenue has been converted to residential use. Bean invented a spray pump that every orchardist had to have. (One of the original models stands, nearly forgotten, outside the Forbes Mill museum.) Bean incorporated in 1904, the year he received his patent, and his grandson John D. Crummey eventually built the Bean Spray Pump Company into the Food Machinery Company, now the conglomerate known as FMC.

Main Street was lined with little wooden buildings when the town was young. Following the Chicago Fire of 1871, growing towns began to require brick construction downtown, but Los Gatos had to learn the hard way. A fire destroyed Seanor's Opera House in 1890, but did not spread. Just two months after a whistle stop visit by President Benjamin Harrison, a disastrous fire on July 26, 1891 swept through the buildings of East Main Street, eventually reaching dynamite stored at the hardware store. Developer Nathan Beckwith learned his lesson and rebuilt the brick Beckwith block which, after extensive earthquake renovations, still stands on East Main Street across from College Avenue. After fire destroyed Lyndon's Los Gatos Hotel in 1898, a fire bell was installed atop a wooden tower across the street. When disaster struck again on October 13, 1901, the wooden tower was burned as well, bringing the new bell crashing to the ground. That fire swept both sides of Main Street from the train tracks to the creek—in modern terms, from Le Boulanger to the freeway.

Urban Growth

March 19, 1904, the electric interurban made its first run from San Jose west on Stevens Creek Boulevard, then the length of Saratoga Avenue, and finally east to Los Gatos. The Opera House that exists today was built by Southern Pacific stationmaster Eugene L. Ford in 1904. The wooden bridge across the creek was replaced in 1905 with a more substantial stone one, which was dedicated just days before the San Francisco earthquake and fire of April 18, 1906. The shock of that catastrophe sent many who could afford it out looking for a calmer way of life, and Los Gatos gained many new residents, among them Richard and Anne Spreckles, distant relatives of the Spreckels Sugar family. They made their home on four acres of Peter Johnson's land and later established a sanitarium at the top of Loma Alta Avenue that is now the Eastfield Ming Quong Conference Center.

Another shaken city dweller was bohemian restaurateur Quintino Ceccanti, who bought an old house on Oak Hill on today's Central Avenue. Ceccanti extended the building, created a garden, grew grapes, made wine, installed mosaic tiles in hand-made fountains and established a fine reputation. He continued making and selling wine during Prohibition in the 1920s (for which he landed in jail several times).

As the town matured, impressive homes were built on Glen Ridge and Bella Vista Avenue. Home & Garden magazine recognized the home of Fairview Plaza developer Frank McCullagh in 1902 after its renovation by famous architect Willis Polk. A permanent Carnegie Library was erected in 1903, and a sturdy Town Hall was built in 1913 on a site that is now the lawn north of today's library. Sunset magazine featured Los Gatos in a 1915 issue, the year that Thomas Edison and Henry Ford visited the town. In 1916, Pacific Gas & Electric unceremoniously destroyed Forbes Mill, leaving only a little annex. J. Walter Crider converted Ford's Opera House into a department store and the Los Gatos Theater was built. It was the end of an era. In 1917, the United States entered the war to end all wars, and in 1918 an influenza epidemic killed half a million Americans. An unexpected downpour caught most of the prune crop in the drying ground trays and cost local businessmen millions of dollars.

In 1920, the first annual Los Gatos Pageant was held. Local celebrity poetess Ruth Comfort Mitchell attended, along with Governor William Stephens. Regular radio broadcasting began in the United States, women won the right to vote, and the first air mail letter was received in Los Gatos. Colonel Erskine Scott Wood and his wife, Sara Bard Field, bought property south of town and commissioned the two famous cat statues as an example of public art. William Weeks' classical high school was built in 1925, and William Crim's First Church of Christ Scientist, which faces it, was completed in 1930.

Some streets in town were paved as early as 1914, but the paving of the Almond Grove neighborhood in 1927 produced a raucous debate between asphalt and concrete advocates. Today's observer will note that concrete won the day. The interurban line was abandoned, and in August 1938, the telephone poles along East Main Street were removed and the lines buried for aesthetic reasons.

The Modern Era

Nothing was the same in America after World War II. Everyone seemed impatient and drive-through food stands and super markets couldn't be built fast enough. California embarked on an ambitious highway program and old San Jose Road (now Los Gatos Boulevard) was too leisurely for the Santa Cruz traffic. The Santa Clara County Water Conservation District, formed when the valley's artesian wells stopped flowing reliably, first dammed Los Gatos Creek at Vasona and then, over great objection, erased the towns of Lexington and Alma under the Lexington Reservoir in 1951.

International Business Machines chose San Jose for a new plant in 1946. "Silicon Valley" began with the transistor in the mid-fifties and took off

1951

1913 Town Hall (Sally Rachel Peters)

with the invention of the integrated circuit in 1959. The fruit economy was replaced as easily as the redwood economy had been earlier.

Throughout the first half of the twentieth century, the town's population was between three and four thousand. The population of Los Gatos increased six fold between 1946 and 1966. The 1913 town hall was replaced with today's modern (yet timeless) center in 1965, and zoning plans encouraged multi-family residential buildings such as the Penthouse Apartments. The train stopped coming after a commemorative run January 25, 1959, and the tracks were torn up a few years later. The town's park, located south of the Main Street bridge and the locus of many fond memories, was displaced by the freeway and replaced by Oak Meadow Park, built by scores of volunteers in 1959. The condemned grammar school on University Avenue was reopened as the Old Town shopping center in 1964.

April 22, 1970, the first "Earth Day," marked a new feeling of environmental awareness. That year, the Los Gatos Scavenger Company changed its name to Green Valley Disposal. *The History of Los Gatos*, published in 1971, reflected a growing awareness that living in the present does not preclude an appreciation of the past. For the nation's bicentennial in 1976, Mardi Bennett organized a cam-

1970

23

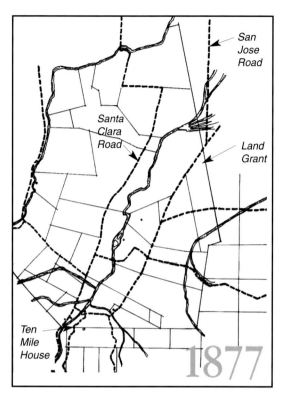

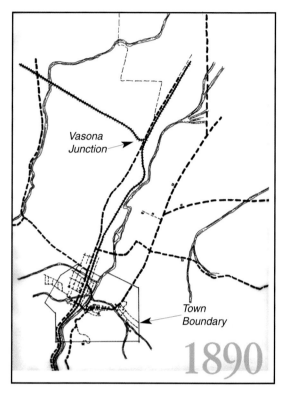

- Farms and orchards.

- Dirt road to Mission Santa Clara (center), San Jose (right).

- 1839 land grant (*Rancho Rinconada de Los Gatos*).

- John Lyndon's Ten Mile House just north of toll gate to Santa Cruz Gap Turnpike.

- Large landowners include (by 1876) Capt. Gardner (244 ac.), Mrs. J. F. Kennedy (356 ac.), John Cilker (174 ac), J. E. Daves (509 ac.) and various members of the Parr family, which owned over 1,200 acres at the north edge of this map.

- Town founded 1887. One square mile centered on Forbes Mill

- Railroad tracks west of creek.Tracks fork toward Saratoga at Vasona Junction.

- Almond Grove and other subdivisions.

- East Main Street is teeming with mercantiles, blacksmiths, newspaper offices.

- Two hotels: John Lyndon's Los Gatos Hotel and the Alpine House (aka Coleman House, aka Rockhaven).

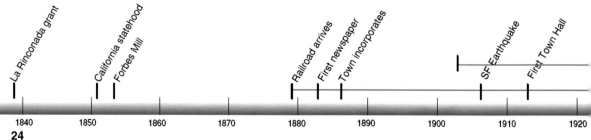

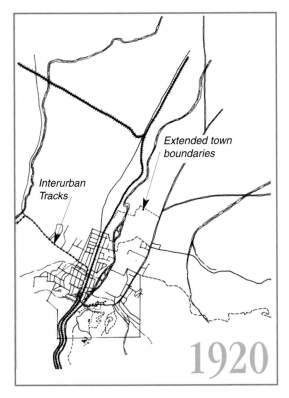

Extended town boundaries

Interurban Tracks

1920

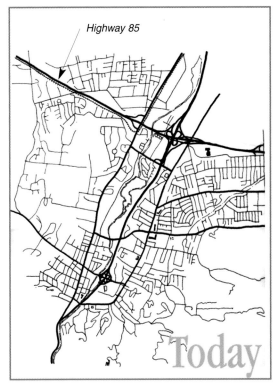

Highway 85

Today

- Interurban railroad from San Jose by way of Saratoga, travels down North Santa Cruz and East Main Street.

- Bunker Hill Park at Main Street bridge renamed Memorial Park after WWI.

- Glenridge Park, Bella Vista, Northside and other neighborhoods developed.

- Wood, Young and Huntington-Perkins estates built in the foothills.

- Many roads paved; home delivery of mail.

- 17 Freeway (1953-57). Creek contained. Town Park moved to Oak Meadow.

- La Rinconada Country Club, Blossom Manor developed.

- County dams creek at Lexington (1952), and Vasona, creating county park (1962).

- Highway 85 (1994) defines north of town.

- Monte Sereno, Saratoga and Campbell incorporated in 1950s.

- Railroad tracks removed (1958)

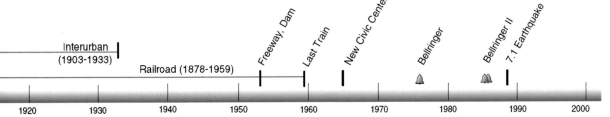

Interurban (1903-1933)
Railroad (1878-1959)
Freeway, Dam
Last Train
New Civic Center
Bellringer
Bellringer II
7.1 Earthquake

1920 1930 1940 1950 1960 1970 1980 1990 2000

paign to restore old homes to their former luster. The cat-shaped doorbells on historic homes throughout town are the result of the Bellringer program (and a follow-up, Bellringer II in 1986-87, coinciding with the town's centennial). The Chart House restaurant chain lovingly restored the Coggeshall mansion in 1976. And Lyndon Plaza finally filled the void left by the destruction of the Lyndon Hotel.

> Why rent when you can buy a 7-room home for $2,250? 3 blocks from schools, $250 down, $25/month.
> —Los Gatos *Times*
> Friday, Nov. 20, 1936

It seems impossible that there is anyone unaware that disaster struck the town of Los Gatos on October 17, 1989, when a magnitude 7.1 earthquake occurred, centered in the hills just south of Lexington. Although Santa Cruz, San Francisco, Oakland, and other communities suffered much more, Los Gatos was badly damaged, too. Many landmark buildings like the La Cañada Building (see 7), the Rankin Block (Le Boulanger, see 5), the Beckwith Block (see 36), and scores of houses were rendered uninhabitable in fourteen or fifteen seconds.

If the quake had hit in the 1960s, there might be no historic buildings still standing in town, but because Los Gatos—and individual owners—took pride in the town's heritage, the important landmarks were rebuilt and restored. Today, the town has not only restored itself, the environment has been improved by projects, such as the Soda Works Plaza (above, left), that, while new, fit in with the town's ambience. Following the earthquake, permit fees were reduced for owners who agreed to rebuild rather than remodel. President Bill Clinton and Vice President Al Gore dined in Los Gatos in June 1993. In recog-

26

nition of over one hundred years of civilization in this corner of the cats, historian William Wulf gave President Clinton a photograph of President Harrison's visit to our town in May 1891. Thanks to a booming economy, the new and antique buildings of Los Gatos have never looked finer.

FRESHLY REMODELED 54 Los Gatos Boulevard (see 62) was severely damaged in the quake.

Praising what is lost makes the remem-brance dear —Shakespeare, "All's Well That Ends Well."

NORTH SANTA CRUZ at Highway 9, looking south, courtesy of Hawkeye Aerial Photography, P. O. Box 449, Santa Clara, CA 95052, (408) 260-0895. Hawkeye has pioneered the use of low-altitude balloon photography for real estate and other purposes.

3 Downtown

WE BEGIN OUR OBSERVATION of Los Gatos at the center: the downtown business district. While the town started on the east bank of the creek, the west bank became open for business in 1857 when the newly-formed Santa Cruz Gap Turnpike Company built their road to Santa Cruz. The road climbed the west side of Los Gatos Canyon and required a bridge across the creek. The road to the bridge, on both sides, became known as Main Street. The railroad chose the west side in 1878 and by the time of the 1891 fire on East Main Street, most of the substantial buildings in town were located near the depot.

CONTENTS

TOWN PLAZA

The town of Los Gatos began as a way station along the trail from San Jose to Santa Cruz. In 1860, a one-room cabin called the Ten Mile House, just south of today's post office, became the area's first hotel. The hotel burned down in 1868 and was rebuilt as a real two-story hotel. Ten years later, when the railroad needed a straight right-of-way into Los Gatos Canyon, John Lyndon bargained for some cash and the relocation of his building across the street. Expanded, remodeled and rebuilt after a 1898 fire, the establishment became the Lyndon Hotel, which faced the depot for 79 years. Lyndon Plaza now occupies the site of the hotel.

The turnpike was a toll road between 1858 and 1877. With a single tollhouse near Lexington, a trip from Los Gatos to Lexington cost as much as the toll to Santa Cruz. Angry citizens complained to the county, which responded in 1867 by insisting upon a two-tier toll, which required that another gate be built in Los Gatos. The owner of the Ten Mile House when the train first arrived was John Weldon Lyndon (1836-1913), a native of Vermont and a

LAWN REPLACED THE TRACKS of the Southern Pacific railroad and depot at the Town Plaza in the mid-1960s.

29

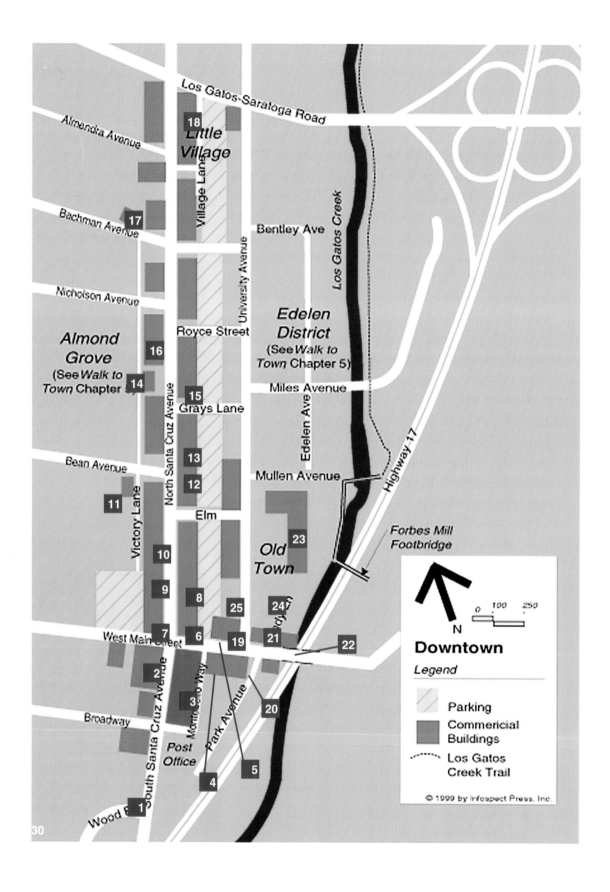

Los Gatos-Saratoga Road

Almendra Avenue

18 Little Village

Bachman Avenue 17

Village Lane

Bentley Ave

Los Gatos Creek

Nicholson Avenue

Almond Grove (See Walk to Town Chapter 14

University Avenue

Royce Street

16

15 Grays Lane

Edelen District (See Walk to Town Chapter 5)

Miles Avenue

Edelen Ave

Bean Avenue

Victory Lane

North Santa Cruz Avenue

13

12

Elm

11

Mullen Avenue

Highway 17

10

9 8

23

Old Town

Forbes Mill Footbridge

7 6

25

24

West Main Street

19 21

22

N

0 100 250

Downtown

Legend

2

Montebello Way

Park Avenue

20

Broadway

3

Post Office

4

5

South Santa Cruz Avenue

1

Wood

Parking

Commericial Buildings

Los Gatos Creek Trail

© 1999 by Infospect Press, Inc.

THE LYNDON HOTEL (left), 1901, replaced the Los Gatos Hotel, destroyed by fire in 1898. John Lyndon died in 1913, but the hotel flourished for decades. It was destroyed in 1963, a few years after the last train visited Los Gatos. **LYNDON PLAZA** (right) was built on the same site. Notice the growth in the surviving palm trees.

successful entrepreneur. The town's second mayor and one of its wealthiest citizens, Lyndon took over day-to-day management of his Los Gatos Hotel after a fire May 26, 1898. Ignoring the town council's objections, he did not build in brick and re-opened as the Lyndon Hotel in 1901.

The center of town activity was the railroad depot located in today's town plaza. President Benjamin Harrison spoke from the train here in May, 1891 and the area was crowded with his audience.

The deodar cedar which the History Club planted across the street from the Lyndon in 1923 has become the town's official Christmas Tree. Permanently strung with lights, the tree is illuminated by the mayor every December to start the annual holiday festivities.

When the last train visited Los Gatos in 1959, the now tired Lyndon Hotel's days were numbered. It was finally razed in 1963, and the town plaza and a modern post office were completed by 1966.

THE FARMER'S MARKET takes over Montebello Way every Sunday morning from 9 a.m. to noon. While it may seem impromptu, the relatively few available spaces make participation an exclusive privilege.

JAMES AND SERENA
KENNEDY DEFEND the toll
house, circa 1876.

FOUR STREET LIGHTS were welded together to display the town's 1899-1949, 1.25-ton fire bell. John Spaur designed the 26' (8m) tall structure, which stands in the Town Plaza at the approximate location of the bell tower which burned in the fire of October 1901.

1 Toll House

HD-73-2

142 South Santa Cruz Avenue
James Kennedy, **1867** Replaced: **1991**

The Santa Cruz Gap Turnpike Company charged tolls for twenty years (1858-1878) to pay for the construction and upkeep of their road to Santa Cruz and in 1867, gatekeeper James Faris Kennedy built a simple house at the gate. The tolls ranged from 50 cents for a single team to $1 for a six-horse team, and the line at the gate sometimes stretched for more than a mile.

Impatient teamsters (wagon drivers), aware that the twenty-year franchise was ending and that the railroad would soon arrive, ripped the gate from its hinges and dumped it into the creek, not once but several times, until the county declared the road public. Kennedy moved out (to land east of Los Gatos Boulevard) in 1877 and the shack became a boarding house. The 97-room Toll House Hotel (William Hedley, Jr., 1983) is adjacent.

Preservationists lost a significant battle in 1991 when the historic single-wall redwood structure was demolished and replaced with a similar building using some original components.

2 Lyndon Plaza

20 South Santa Cruz Avenue
Jack Austin (Developer), Dennis Robza (Project Architect), **1978**

This contemporary two-story commercial court was built on the site of the storied Lyndon Hotel, demolished in 1963. The Lyndon Hotel emerged in 1901 from the partially burned Los Gatos Hotel, which was also owned by prominent town father John Lyndon. Palm trees planted in 1901 have survived and now tower above the modern Italianate low-pitched mansard roof. (Photo on page 31.)

3 Town Plaza

South Santa Cruz Avenue & West Main Street, **1965**

The Town Plaza was built on the site of the railroad depot, one hundred years after the construction of the town's first hotel, the Ten Mile House. The railroad was here 1878-1959, 81 years.

The plaza originally had two fountains (the missing one was closer to Main Street). The two main buildings facing the south end of the park were built just after it: The General Telephone building in 1965 and the U. S. Post Office in 1966.

The town plaza is used for outdoor concerts sponsored by the town's Arts Commission and as the embarkation point for horse-drawn carriage rides during the holiday season. Every Sunday morning, Montebello Way becomes a pedestrian farmer's market.

http://amicis.com/wwwsys/LEBOUL/leboul6.location.html

4 Rankin Block HD-76-2
145 West Main Street
Clara Rankin, **1902** Restoration: John Lien, **1991**

Built after the fire of October 1901 which destroyed the Wilcox Block (Commercial Bank Building) on this site by Clara Rankin, the first woman member of the local Chamber of Commerce, the Rankin Block housed the Chamber (1922-1989) and the Post Office (1917-1948). The Johns & Johnson Drug Store occupied the corner where Le Boulanger is today, facing the Watkins-Skinkle drug store under the La Cañada turret.

Damaged in the 1989 earthquake, the building required extensive structural repair by developer Ian Macrae.

MUSIC IN THE PLAZA, an eclectic series of free Sunday afternoon concerts, has become a summer tradition.

LE BOULANGER (the baker) offers a sweet respite for footsore observers of the downtown scene in the historic Rankin Block.

5 First National Bank

160 West Main Street
1920 Restoration: Homestead Savings (sponsor), **1973**

Built by the First National Bank, this exquisite Renaissance Revival building served the bank until its closure in 1955.

Town historian Clarence Hamsher was a director of the bank, founded in 1911, and its cashier. He collected newspaper clippings and old photographs of the town which were donated to the library after his death in the 1950s. Dr. Bruntz used C. F. Hamsher's files for his 1971 *History of Los Gatos* and dedicated his work to the pioneering volunteer historian.

VALERIANO'S RISTORANTE is the latest in a series of restaurants in the First National Bank Building.including the London Oyster Room and Il Nido (the nest). Valeriano's offers fine dining in a wonderful atmosphere. Be sure to notice the original bank vault to the right of the front door.

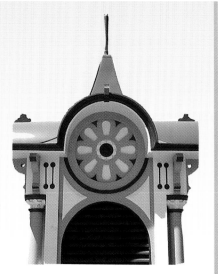

THE FARWELL BUILDING, 223 West Main, developed by Sue Farwell, designed by Michael McKay, will be completed in 1999. Controversy surrounded the requested return of the cupola (right) from the home of Farwell's father-in-law's great uncle James Lyndon. The cupola, donated to the town, is slated instead for a new bandstand in Oak Meadow Park.

AMERICAN CRAFTS, art which emphasizes natural materials and sometimes native American themes, is on display at the Twig gallery in the Park Vista Building. The store, which has a sister in San Francisco, features products ranging from jewelry to furniture to lamps to frames.

6 Park Vista Building
2 North Santa Cruz Avenue
Bank of America, **1931**

In the early months of the Great Depression, the Bank of America erected this elegant Italian edifice with its art deco bas relief panels. The forty year old Theresa Block—built by John Lyndon in 1890 and named for his wife, Theresa Rector—was demolished in the process. The site became known as the bank corner because the Bank of Los Gatos had always faced the intersection and Bank of America continued the tradition. The area changed dramatically in 1963 when the adjacent railroad tracks were removed, the depot became the Town Plaza and the Lyndon Hotel was razed. B of A built a new, more suburban, branch bank at 333 North Santa Cruz. The building was restored after damage in the 1989 earthquake.

BAS-RELIEF panels include symbols for architecture and medicine, apparently to honor the bank's upstairs tenants.

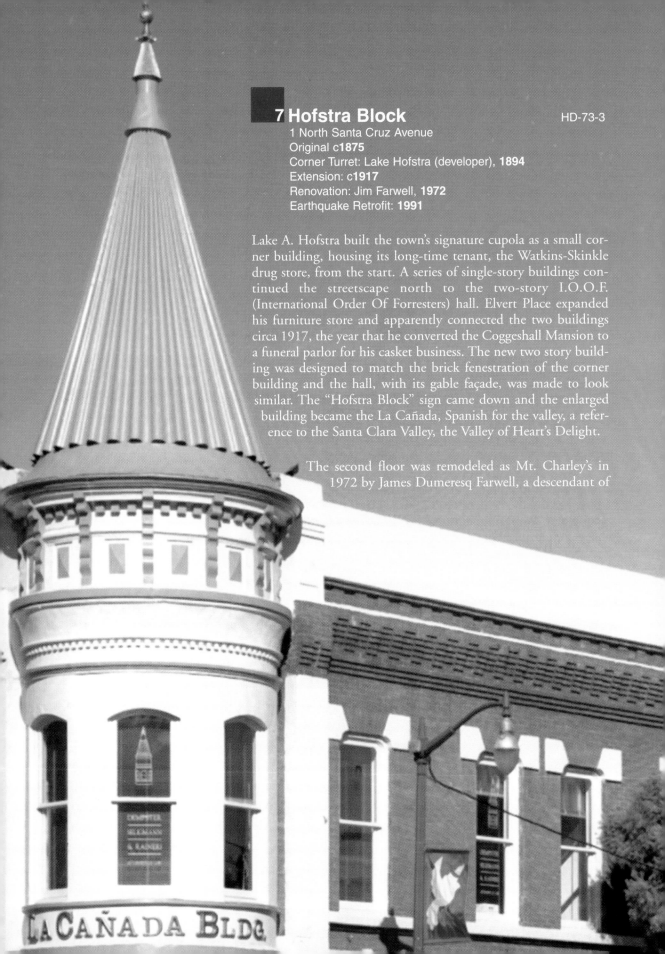

7 Hofstra Block

HD-73-3

1 North Santa Cruz Avenue
Original c**1875**
Corner Turret: Lake Hofstra (developer), **1894**
Extension: c**1917**
Renovation: Jim Farwell, **1972**
Earthquake Retrofit: **1991**

Lake A. Hofstra built the town's signature cupola as a small corner building, housing its long-time tenant, the Watkins-Skinkle drug store, from the start. A series of single-story buildings continued the streetscape north to the two-story I.O.O.F. (International Order Of Forresters) hall. Elvert Place expanded his furniture store and apparently connected the two buildings circa 1917, the year that he converted the Coggeshall Mansion to a funeral parlor for his casket business. The new two story building was designed to match the brick fenestration of the corner building and the hall, with its gable façade, was made to look similar. The "Hofstra Block" sign came down and the enlarged building became the La Cañada, Spanish for the valley, a reference to the Santa Clara Valley, the Valley of Heart's Delight.

The second floor was remodeled as Mt. Charley's in 1972 by James Dumeresq Farwell, a descendant of

LA CAÑADA BLDG.

both John Lyndon and James Bacigalupi, the first president of the Bank of America. It was apparently during this renovation that the turret lost its tiny, curvaceous ballustrade.

The 1989 earthquake was disastrous for the cupola and the Farwell and Bacigalupi families sponsored repairs and a seismic retrofit led by James Farwell. Active with the high school and a member of the Historic Preservation Commission, James Farwell tragically succumbed to cancer in 1992 at the age of 49.

THEN AS NOW, the corner of Main and Santa Cruz bustles with activity. In 1895, the commercial district extended only as far as the Cannery at 57 North Santa Cruz (extreme right in photo). The block was "filled in" in 1917 as the shops pushed northward. The corner drug store (Watkins-Skinkle) was a fixture under the turret for 80 years. What looks like a hovering UFO is an electric street lamp.

NORTH SANTA CRUZ

The half-mile (762 m) stretch of North Santa Cruz Avenue from Main Street to Saratoga Road comprises the town's core commercial district. At the turn of the century, the business district was little more than the buildings which faced the train depot. North Santa Cruz was bounded by the Los Gatos Cannery (1882-1906), a thriving complex about where the Los Gatos Theater is today. The west side of the street north of Bean Avenue was lined with elegant mansions. Commercial development replaced all but the Coggeshall home (now the Chart House restaurant).

Several buildings downtown feature styling first exhibited at the Exposition Internationale des Arts Decoratifs et Industriels Modernes in Paris in 1925. The popular style, known as "Art Deco," features streamlined ornaments, speed lines, and American Indian and Mayan zigzags. There are four art deco buildings downtown: the theater 10 (remodeled 1929), Park Vista 6 (1931) the Gem City Laundry 25 (remodeled 1932) and the Peerless Stage Depot 16 (1938), which interprets the style in colorful ceramic tile.

8 Bogart Hardware
18 North Santa Cruz Avenue
1906

Arthur Wellington Bogart owned hardware stores in San Francisco, San Jose and this one in Los Gatos, where the Bogart family spent their summers. Shortly after Arthur's death, his wife Jemima built an estate in the hills west of Glenridge (see 109) and their nephew, Mr. Templeman, acquired the store. The Boy's Club (1907-1911) and the Woodmen of the World met in the hall upstairs. In 1972, the ground floor became the Los Gatos Variety Store and it is now one of Steve Diddam's four Amazing Party Stores.

The Strand. 2 shows nightly at 7:30 and 9:00. Tonight: Doug Fairbanks in *Bound in Morocco*. The admirers of Doug will find this picture one of the most delightful of productions. As a loose-fisted, sharp-tongued American runs amuck in the Sultan's harem, saves the Queen, bust up— Oh! What's the use? You know Doug Fairbanks. Children 11¢, Adults 22¢.

9 Crall's Stationery
21 North Santa Cruz Avenue
c1916

Crall's Stationery, a four-generation family business founded by Henry J. and continued by Henry C., Henry L. and his sons, Henry Christopher and Craig William (see 75) closed in 1981, but the original mosaic vestibule remains.

Started in smaller quarters across the street (6 North Santa Cruz), Andale (fast) has become a four-store chain with branches in Palo Alto and San Francisco. The restaurant design is stunning, particularly the confident use of bold and muted colors inside and out. Notice the three-dimensional mural depicting a windstorm, and don't overlook the delightful patio in the rear.

http://www.cameracinemas.com

10 Los Gatos Theater
41 North Santa Cruz Avenue
J. A. Marshall (developer), **1916**

Built as a 600-seat silent movie house (complete with a Wurlitzer organ), this town lanmark was originally part of a block of shops in a plain Renaissance Revival building. The flat marquee had a glass fringe, and it has been known as the Premier and the Strand as well as the Los Gatos Theater. The Art Deco style, knife blade neon sign and pop-out marquee were added after a September 1929 fire.

Heavily damaged by the 1989 earthquake, the movie house did not reopen until 1993 after the present owners had remodeled the layout into two, 200-seat theaters featuring primarily artistic and critically-acclaimed films. The new auditoriums are wider than they are deep, which is said to offer a more intimate cinematic experience.

ONE OF SOME 33 retail stores featuring the upscale garden equipment purveyed by catalog merchant Smith & Hawken (26 North Santa Cruz), founded in 1981. Open-air vestibules handle the transition from the street.

THE GAP at 120 North Santa Cruz allows shoppers to walk through to the parking lot. The train tracks which paralleled Santa Cruz Avenue were replaced by parking in the 1960s.

A MOTION PICTURE show made a fine excuse for a trip to town. Advertisement (opposite) from the February 20, 1919 issue of the *Mail-News*.

39

11 Mail-News Building
213 Bean Avenue
Russell Sund (builder), **1929**

Hiland Baggerly, a veteran newspaperman from the big city, came to Los Gatos in 1927 and bought the *Mail-News*. He commissioned this Mediterranean Revival building which served the paper until its demise in 1953. Hi Baggerly successfully defended the newspaper against a libel suit brought by a judge who did not like his leniency in a drunk driving case held up to public scrutiny. Local columnist John Baggerly is Hiland's son.

The Los Gatos Museum on Tait Avenue, built in 1927 also by Russell Sund, offers the same sunny blend of Mission simplicity and Spanish Colonial wrought iron. The Mail-News building features one shed, one flat and one gable roof, and observers can't miss the polychromatic tile stair.

12 Cotton Works
58 N Santa Cruz Ave
Chris Spaulding, **1991**

A beautiful example of sparse design, the Cotton Works was one of developer Dave Flick's first forays into commercial work. The minimalist details are rich, including subtle stone mouldings and Old World copper drainspouts.

13 Lawson Plumbing and Sheet Metal Shop
112-116 North Santa Cruz Avenue
c**1918**

What appears to be rusticated stone on the south wall of Louis H. Lawson's Plumbing and Sheet Metal Shop is actually stamped metal.

14 Coggeshall Mansion

HD-75-6

115 North Santa Cruz Avenue
J. J. Hill (builder), **1891** Renovation: **1976**

Mary G. Coggeshall, native of Australia and widow of B. S. Coggeshall, built this house in 1891 for herself and her children, Russell and Geneva. Second-generation undertaker and furniture salesman Elvert Ernest Place converted the house to a mortuary in 1917, which it remained until 1976, when the building was beautifully renovated as a Chart House restaurant.

The Chart House chain was founded in Aspen, Colorado in 1961 by surfer Joey Cabell and Navy frogman Buzzy Bent. Bent vowed that "no Chart House site would be ordinary, no building—new or old—less than special." More than twenty-four Chart House restaurants, including this one, occupy buildings deemed significant by historical organizations.

Mrs. Coggeshall's home is a classic Queen Anne structure with a round turret and asymmetrical massing. The wraparound porch features a circular lattice and decorative spindlework.

FUNERAL HOME is now a well-preserved restaurant.

15 Los Gatos Brewing Company

130 North Santa Cruz Avenue
c**1928** Renovation: **1991**

Built as an automobile service garage for Watson Poole, this building housed Paul Swanson Ford in 1940. Used cars were sold from a lot to the north, and the service bays were at the rear of the building, which backed up to the railroad tracks.

The building was extensively remodeled as a micro-brewery. Shops occupy the former car showroom, and the service department is now a dining room. The LGB model train company of Germany sued over the Brewing Company's logo, but the restaurant won. Amy Konsterlie's watercolors of Los Gatos adorn the dining room.

Los Gatos Brewing Company

16 Peerless Stage Depot

133-145 North Santa Cruz Avenue
J. C. Monk (builder), **1938**

Peerless buses carried passengers to Santa Cruz after train service was discontinued in the late 1930s. Unusual green tiles and Art Deco motifs decorate the one-story building. The tiles manage to achieve both rhythm and relief on an essentially flat façade.

C. B. HANNEGAN'S—Think Irish barbeque.

17 C. B. Hannegan's
208 Bachman Avenue
c**1890**, First floor added: **1940**

Chris Benson and John Hannegan created their unique restaurant in 1980. Hannegan, a former manager at Mt. Charley's, is involved with the sister city program which pairs San Jose with Dublin, Ireland. (Los Gatos' sister city is Listowel, a suburb of Dublin.) Hannegan and former mayor Patrick O'Laughlin have been known to celebrate St. Patrick's Day by hosting Irish visitors at C. B. Hannegan's. The house in the rear was built circa 1890 and was raised in the air in 1940 and a new first floor built underneath it.

In the chaotic hours following the 1989 earthquake, Chris Benson personally barbecued food—over 2,000 meals were served in two days—on the restaurant's huge portable grill for emergency workers and others in the mostly blacked-out town.

HOUSE OF HANSEL AND GRETEL Candy Store at 340 North Santa Cruz, now a restaurant, was designed by L. Rath in 1947. Most of the Black Forest decorations have been stripped away, but the exaggerated proportions make it an interesting example of the storybook architecture of the Little Village.

18 Little Village Shops
300-350 North Santa Cruz Avenue
1945-1950

Realtor Effie V. Walton (1884-1969) built the quaint shops along Village and Petticoat Lane. Prior to 1889, the site had been the town cemetery. Effie and her husband Arthur (1882-1960) were in show business together in the 1910s and 1920s. The couple helped develop Aldercroft Heights, a neighborhood in the Santa Cruz Mountains, in the 1930s. Effie served two terms as president of the Los Gatos Chamber of Commerce and later wrote *Two for the Show* about her marriage and other successes. Effie, the first woman president of the Chamber, was apparently a strong role model for women—her husband is listed in one town directory as a salesman at "Mrs. E. V. Walton Realty."

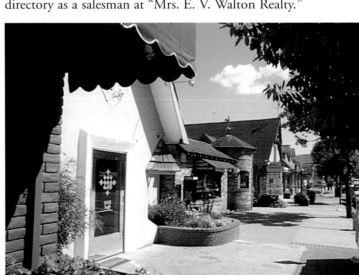

MAIN STREET

The main street in a town that does not yet have streets must lead to the bridge across the creek. The wooden bridge built in 1857 was replaced in 1882 and 1906. The latter was dedicated a matter of days before the San Francisco earthquake and was a graceful stone and concrete design that would have stood proudly for a hundred years had it not been destroyed as part of the Highway 17 construction in 1954. The creek has been spanned at this location since the 1840s.

Before the fire of October 1901, wooden buildings overlooked the creek at the west end of the bridge. The Arlington Hotel, on the north side of the street, featured a dining room below street level with large windows facing the creek and the sound of the rushing water. A reading room, the forerunner of the Los Gatos Public Library, was established in the L. A. Wilder store on the south side of Main Street on March 4, 1898. The first library hung over the creek on stilts.

NOT VERY DIFFERENT from today, the photograph below was likely taken in the late 1920s. From left, the First National Bank (5), Crider's Department Store (the Opera House, 19), and the Fretwell Building (21) are clearly visible. Across the 1906 stone bridge, the white scalloped building (far right) is the Baptist Church, demolished in 1958 to make way for the Penthouse Apartments. There was no Highway 17, but notice the crossing gates at the far left—the tracks of the Southern Pacific crossed the interurban trolley tracks at this point.

Main St. - Los Gatos, Calif.

http://www.operahousebanquets.com

19 Ford's Opera House   HD-75-5
140 West Main Street
1904
Façade: c**1940**
Renovation:Sal Caruso, **1989**

Depot agent Eugene Long Ford (1857-1909) bought the site of the Parr Block, destroyed by the fire of October 1901, from Mrs. Mary Parr for ten dollars. His 500-seat Opera House, featuring stamped tin panels on the ceiling and the upper walls, was inaugurated by the *Sweet Clover* company, which gave the opening performance in October 1904. The Opera House became a fixture on the traveling chatauqua and theater circuit. Young Henry Crall, son of the owner of Crall's Stationers next door (later on Santa Cruz Avenue), served as manager.

In 1916, J. Walter Crider (see 104) established a Dry Goods Store (later Crider's Department Store) in the building that operated until 1957. An unfortunate "modernization," which hid the Victorian façade behind rectangular panels, was applied in 1940 and rescinded in the early 1990s. The Opera House is available for meetings, events and weddings.

THE ARTHUR BERRYMAN BUILDING at 78 West Main, 1908.

http://www.losgatoscoffeeroasting.com

20 Los Gatos Coffee Roasting Company
101 West Main Street
1909-10
Renovation: Gifford Sobey, **1950**

Teri Hope (see 70) created the town's premier hang-out, the Los Gatos Coffee Roasting Company, in 1982, long before Starbuck's or even micro-breweries were as popular as they are now. Her success led to coffee roasting stores in Carmel, Palo Alto and elsewhere and to volunteer work with organizations such as the Teen Counseling Center of the West Valley and the Los Gatos Chamber of Commerce.

21 Fretwell Building
98 West Main Street
1906

Jeweler J. J. Fretwell (see 28) built this building just after the new main street bridge was completed. Like the bridge, the building is made of concrete, but here the material is made to look like cut stone. The round arches signal an example of Romanesque, a style popularized on the east coast by influential architect Henry Hobson Richardson.

The Fretwell building housed the First National Bank from 1912 to 1918 when the bank moved to 160 West Main (see 5).

22 Montezuma Block
14 West Main Street
1902, Housing conversion: **1941**

The Montezuma Block was built after the 1901 fire destroyed the Arlington Hotel on this site. The Foothill Hotel (actually more of a boarding house) operated above the shops, but the storefronts were closed up in 1941 when the building was converted to wartime housing. The building has housed a saloon, a butcher shop, a movie theater and the town Post Office (1902-17).

FOOTHILL HOTEL: $1.50 single, $3.50 double with bath. (1925 town directory.)

OLD TOWN

The Old Town area includes the newly remodeled retail center bisected by University Avenue as well as the unique stone Craftsman bungalow and the venerable St. Luke's. Old Town is an inside joke. It was never the old part of town—the grammar school existed on this site from 1881 until the 1950s. School Street became University Avenue when the little schoolhouse was replaced by a full-fledged grammar school.

http://www.oakvillegrocery.com
http://www.calcafe.com/losgatos
http://www.borders.com/stores/192

23 **Old Town**   HR-4
50 University Avenue
Wyckoff & White, **1923**
Frank Laulainen, **1964**
William Hagman, **1998-99**

This land was purchased for a school from the Mullen family in 1881. The present building is the third grammar school, constructed in 1923 after the old building was sold to the San Francisco Wrecking Company. Louise Van Meter taught in room 2A of the two-story 1885 building, and a high school was added to the facility in 1894. (A new high school was built on East Main in 1908.) By 1920, burgeoning enrollment and aging facilities forced the construction of a new school.

The new facility was styled after the mission at San Juan Capistrano, with a long colonnade of arches and an auditorium with a bell tower. In April 1926, the school bought land across the creek and a low, swinging bridge was built to connect with a new playground next to Forbes Mill Annex. The Highway

THE LITTLE THEATER (below), originally the 1923 grammar school's auditorium, is now a bookstore.

46

THE CALIFORNIA CAFE features interiors designed by the Engstrom Design Group. Bill Clinton and Al Gore dined at the California Café in 1993.

Department was obliged, as a matter of policy, to replace this bridge in 1954 when Highway 17 was built, which is why a steel pedestrian bridge crosses the freeway today.

The school was closed due to seismic concerns in the late 1950s, and, in 1964, far-sighted Berkeley developer Max Walden (and partner William Rinehart) remodeled the derelict school into a shopping center, one of the first historic renovations for commercial purposes in California. Walden was 39 and explained that he had been inspired by Copenhagen's well-designed Tivoli Gardens. (Walt Disney admitted that Tivoli inspired Disneyland, as well.) Walden and his local architect, Frank Laulainen, had plans to link downtown and remote parking with a trolley, and made a proposal to rebuild the historic Lyndon Hotel. In the end, Old Town was the extent of the project and Walden moved to Santa Cruz and renovated historic buildings there.

President Bill Clinton and Vice President Al Gore dined at Old Town in June 1993. Hunter/Storm of Cupertino, owners of fourteen Bay Area shopping centers, bought the property in February 1995 for $3.7 million and are completing an ambitious $15 million renovation which extends the facility across University Avenue (see "New Old Town," next page).

THE NEW UNIVERSITY Avenue Grammar School shortly after its completion in 1923. The orignial building and the high school wing had been adjacent to the street, but now that automobiles were here, the new facility kept its distance.

24 St. Luke's Episcopal Church
20 University Avenue
W. Dolhim, **1901-03**
Expansion: **1954**

Theresa Rector, wife of John Lyndon, donated the property for an Episcopal church in 1882, but the wooden structure, one of the earliest churches in town, was destroyed in the fire of October 1901. Mrs. Thomas Evans, Mary McCullagh's mother, was visiting as a new church was contemplated and when she returned to her home in Gemantown, Pennsylvania, she organized her church, St. Luke's, to raise funds for the Los Gatos parish. Grateful Los Gatans named the church, designed by San Francisco architect W. Dolhim, after their benefactors in Pennsylvania. The mission style building was built by local contractor Hy Hooper, and painted by local resident Jack Sullivan.

The parking lot south of the church was the site of the Carnegie Library (1903-1953) and the church facility was expanded after the library was destroyed.

NEW OLD TOWN is built over subterranean parking on the Sterling Lumber site. William Hagman's interesting mix of forms and bold but tasteful color palette contrasts favorably with less successful commercial architecture in town.

http://steamers-restaurant.com
http://www.gap.com

25 Stone House & Gem City Laundry
15 & 11 University Avenue
1906
Herman Bauman, **1930**

A Craftsman bungalow in stone (on a wood frame), the house at 15 University was built by Charles Wagner, a Main Street barber. Mrs. Alice Wagner operated a photo studio here in 1912. In 1930, the Libante family moved here from Johnson Avenue and relocated their French Laundry into a new Art Deco building that they built next door (at 11 University).

A French Laundry (known for painstaking work cleaning lace and fine fabrics, the way that a Chinese Laundry is known for starched shirts), the building is one of three examples of Art Deco downtown. The architect, Herman Bauman, was a prolific designer of apartment buildings in San Francisco.

Gem City Laundry, now In the Olde Manner.

A CASUALTY OF THE EARTH-QUAKE, the original stone chimney (left of the dormer on the right) was not replaced.

LOS GATOS UNION HIGH SCHOOL

THEY DID IT RIGHT when William Weeks'
Greek Revival high school was built in 1925.
They bought and demolished all the wooden
stores and houses in the way of a grand lawn
and planted a line of stately palm trees, creating
a thing of beauty for future generations.

4 Civic Center

The Civic Center district, East Main Street and surroundings, includes the offices of the Town of Los Gatos, the High School, foothill homes and the Johnson district, up the gentle rise to the east once known as El Monte hill.

Los Gatos was established here, on the east bank of the creek, by Forbes' Mill and Buffalo Jones' lumber yard in the 1850s, where the road from San Jose turned left to follow the creek up to Jones' redwood mill. A proper bridge crossed the creek in 1857 to connect San Jose with the new Santa Cruz Turnpike, although makeshift bridges had existed here since the early 1840s. The bridge defined the budding town's "main street."

East Main Street was a thriving downtown, teeming with mercantiles, blacksmiths, hotels and saloons in wooden buildings with wooden sidewalks until the fire of July, 1891. The fire was fueled by the dry buildings and the merchandise in stores such as the Place & Fretwell Furniture and Undertaking establishment, where the fire began. When the flames found dynamite stored in the Los Gatos Store, the explosion broke glass a half-mile away. The fire spurred development on the west side, including the Hofstra Block (today's La Cañada Building).

Urban renewal came to East Main Street in 1925, when dozens of buildings were demolished to give the new high school its grand lawn. And again in 1965, when several businesses and the old Town Hall and tiny Town Jail were razed in favor of the new civic center.

CONTENTS

THE FIRST DOWNTOWN, East Main Street now hosts the civic center and high school along with shops and restaurants.

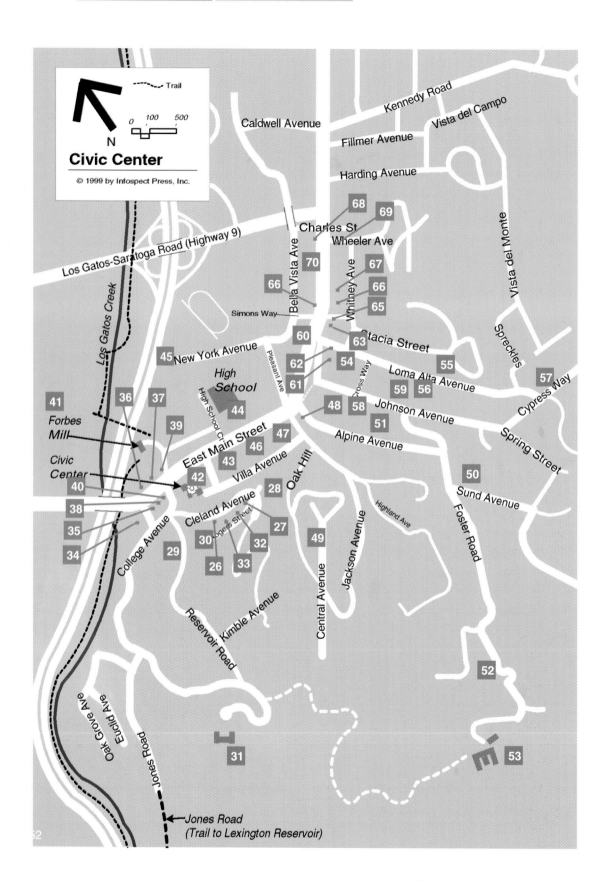

Civic Center

Trail

N

0 100 500

Caldwell Avenue

Kennedy Road

Fillmer Avenue

Vista del Campo

Harding Avenue

Los Gatos-Saratoga Road (Highway 9)

Charles St

Wheeler Ave

68

69

Bella Vista Ave

70

67

66

66

65

Whitney Ave

Simons Way

Los Gatos Creek

45   New York Avenue

High School

High School Ct

Pleasant Ave

60

62

61

63

Stacia Street

54

Cross Way

Loma Alta Avenue

55

Spreckles

57

Vista del Monte

Cypress Way

41

36

37

39

Forbes Mill

Civic Center

40

38

35

34

College Avenue

44

East Main Street

47

46

43

42

28

Villa Avenue

Cleland Avenue

Rogers Street

30

26   33

32

27

29

Reservoir Road

Kimble Avenue

Oak Hill

49

Central Avenue

Jackson Avenue

Highland Ave

48   58

51

Alpine Avenue

Johnson Avenue

59   56

50

Sund Avenue

Foster Road

Spring Street

52

31

53

Oak Grove Ave

Euclid Ave

Jones Road

Jones Road
(Trail to Lexington Reservoir)

COLLEGE

The College area is named for the Jesuit college known as the Novitiate, built on the north face of Jones (now St. Joseph's) Hill. The wagon track to Jones' mill still exists—Jones Road is partially domesticated, with paving and houses, but mostly it's a public trail leading to Lexington Reservoir.

Three grand homes look down on College at 33, 35, and 39. The house at number 33 may be the A. E. Ellis House, which dates to 1871, making it the oldest house in town according to town records. Number 39 was built in 1887 and features eleven and a half foot (3.5m) ceilings. A campaign button for William Jennings Bryan was found in the attic. Private steps are built into the mortarless rock wall at the street.

Wilcox Road led from East Main Street to the lands of Harvey Wilcox, who sold thirty-nine acres, twelve hundred orange trees and a vineyard to the Society of Jesus on March 18, 1886. The Jesuits completed their first college in April 1888 and expanded for the next 90 years.

Water from Los Gatos Creek had been diverted for use by Forbes Mill as early as 1854 on the west side, but in 1870, a flume was built on the east, along Jones Trail (portions of which still exist). The flume fed a cistern (which also still exists) above the mill, which gives Reservoir Road its name.

The rise east of the reservoir has been called Tarantula Flats, but the origin of the name is elusive. Gopher trap magnate Zephyr Macabee, who parceled off lots to his friends in the early 20th century, once owned the entire hill.

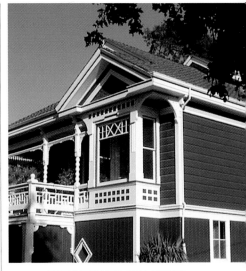

THE HEIGHTS OF LOWER College Avenue overlook downtown. This home at 39 College was built in 1887 for John J. King, one of the town's first dentists, and remodeled in 1907. The four bedroom house features a den in the rear. The bay window was filled by a brass bed in the 1970s, because the owners enjoyed stargazing.

ALL THAT REMAINS of the Los Gatos Hotel and Saloon, which burned in 1968, is the intricate brick wall on College at East Main Street (HD-73-12). Luigi Mariotti, who bought the hotel in 1904, commissioned an Italian stonemason to build the wall in 1910, in order to link the hotel with the Puccinelli residence (now the Tapestry bistro) and the carriage house (later the Los Gatos Soda Works). The wall was to have encircled the property, but a death in the family sent the mason home to Italy and the project was never completed.

53

Cleland House

26 Cleland House

90 Cleland Avenue
William Cleland, **1875**

William Cleland, a 36-year-old Hoosier, bought property on the bluff overlooking Los Gatos in 1874, well before the train arrived or the town was incorporated. He built the first house on this site in 1875. His son, Thomas S. Cleland, teamed with George, the son of town pioneer Dr. W. S. McMurtry and together they operated the Los Gatos Store on East Main Street. The current owner of the house clearly has eclectic tastes; notice the Japanese torii gate in the backyard.

27 Stanfield House

126 Cleland Avenue
John Stanfield, **1885**

John J. Stanfield (1834-1894) grew oranges and grapes on 261 acres south of San Jose. Born in Ireland, he had arrived in San Francisco in 1858. He was a founding shareholder in the Bank of Los Gatos in November 1883 and built this house about 1885. From the upper floor, he might have been able to keep an eye on his bank near today's Ferrari dealer.

John's son James was born on the family farm in 1862 and lived in this house when he married Phoebe S. Fretwell. Their son, John Harold, was born here in 1893. The next year, James, now a Vice President at the Bank, was elected Town Treasurer for a two-year term. James, Phoebe and James' sister Helen lived in the house. James was elected to the town council in 1914, meeting in the brand new Town Hall at Main Street and Seanor Avenue (now Pageant Way). The family sold this house in 1916. James became the equivalent of Mayor in 1918, but abruptly resigned the council in 1919, sold the family orchard and vineyard and moved away. When the family returned, in 1922, they settled at 101 Glenridge.

Ralph Phillips, Chief of Police (1943-1970), also lived in this house, which has been beautifully restored and improved in recent years.

28 Fretwell House
3 Kimble Avenue
J. J. Fretwell, **1891**

Joseph J. Fretwell's sister Phoebe lived at 126 Cleland with her husband J. J. Stanfield when Joseph built this home in 1891. Fretwell was in partnership with the town undertaker, Elvert Place, in a furniture and coffin-making company on East Main Street at the time. In the early hours of Monday, July 27, 1891, Fretwell, like the rest of the town, was probably alerted by the ringing of the bell at the Presbyterian Church to a fire that started in a wooden building behind the Place & Fretwell store. The store, and eight other businesses, were totally destroyed.

Fretwell recovered from the fire and in 1906 built the masonry building at the corner of Main and University that bears his name (see 21).

Joseph Fretwell house.

30 Lelia P. Dyer House
Reservoir Road?
Bernard Maybeck, **1910**

We conclude that Mrs. Lelia P. Dyer commissioned a house from famed architect Bernard Maybeck in February 1910. Maybeck (1862-1957) designed craftsman cottages, practically inventing the Berkeley Style at the turn of the century, and larger commissions as well, including the building that now houses San Francisco's Exploratorium. Maybeck's records were destroyed in the 1906 earthquake, so it is difficult to prove that he worked in Los Gatos prior, but we know that he designed a residence for "L. P. Dyer" in Los Gatos in 1910. We also know that Leila Dyer lived on Reservoir Road in 1919 and that this house appeared between 1908 and 1928. The exact whereabouts of the Dyer house remain a mystery, however.

20TH CENTURY TEA & GROCERY merchant Harrison David "Harry" Baumgardner's house at 120 Cleland. Harry (1875-1965) was also the druggist at the Watkins-Skinkle corner drug store (1912-1922). Born in Zaneville, Ohio, he arrived in Los Gatos in 1885. Perhaps his father is the Mr. Baumgartner credited with construction of the original novitiate.

29 Bound Brook

10 Reservoir Road
W. D. Tisdale, **1891**

William DeWitt Tisdale (1845-98) brought a large vision with him from San Jose. Associated with quartz mining in Nevada County, California, and one of the founders of the First National Bank of San Jose in 1874, Tisdale formed the Los Gatos Ice Works at Forbes Mill in 1885 and the San Jose Electric Improvement Company in 1889. Tisdale was personally responsible for installing the first electric streetlight in town (located approximately where Valeriano's is today) on January 31, 1891, with power generated at the Los Gatos Manufacturing Company (Forbes Mill). He served as president of San Jose Water Company 1894-1896.

Tisdale built his three-story mansion for his wife Luella and their four children (Bettie, John, Robert and Blanche) just below the flume (the "bound brook") supplying the cistern that gives Reservoir Road its name. A large-scaled Queen Anne, the house is decorated with an unusual artichoke plant motif and a repeated pattern of squares and rectangles in the generous wainscoting and elsewhere. The turret faces northwest toward town and features expansive curved glass double-hung windows.

The two-acre property also includes a camp-style, two-story cabin and a Mediterranean Revival concrete swimming pool and cabana. (Unbridled speculation, to be sure, but Bernard Maybeck dabbled in the peeled log "camp" style, and it is therefore vaguely possible that the cabin is the missing Lelia P. Dyer house.)

CONCRETE SWIMMING POOL, temporarily empty, dates to the 1920s.

CARPENTER GOTHIC detailing on the northwest corner. Notice the beautiful gable end in particular.

CAMP-STYLE peeled-log fireplace mantel may be the lost L. P. Dyer House.

WRITING DESK with an overview of the heart of Los Gatos from the curved glass windows in the huge turret.

57

MIRASSOU CHAMPAGNE Cellars operates at the Novitiate, selling wine and hosting special event dinners and brunches.

Gate motifs include grapes, plants and religious symbols.

31 Sacred Heart Jesuit Center
300 College Avenue
Harry Baumgartner (original builder), **1888**

The grand white structure on the hill, a visible presence available from most streets in town by simply lifting one's gaze, is known as the Novitiate. (A novitiate houses novices, "persons admitted to probationary membership in a religious community.")

The Society of Jesus has been in the west since 1591, and the school for priests has been here since the town's founding. The original building, a four-story, Empire-style brick schoolhouse, lasted eighty years. Wings added in 1914 and 1926 remain—the central building was replaced in 1968-69 by an unfortunate five-story glass curtain wall with a folded-plate roof.

The priests extended Harvey Wilcox's original 1881 vineyard and rebuilt the winery in 1896, the cellar of which remains, and pressed sacramental wine throughout Prohibition. The property holdings grew steadily to almost 400 acres, and the order purchased land near Bear Creek Road as well. Jones Hill was re-christened St. Joseph's Hill, probably to honor the first church in San Jose (built in 1803), which was named for the patron saint of the Mission Santa Clara. Future governor Edmund G. "Jerry" Brown, Jr. (1938-), son of the state's then attorney general and later governor, attended the seminary in the late 1950s.

The school became a retirement home for Jesuit priests and, in November 1979, ceased cultivation of the renowned vineyards.

32 Ryland House

36 Rogers Street
Frank Lobdell, **1888** Remodeling: Chris Spaulding, **1985-99**

Joseph R. Ryland, a rich man's son, would have only the best. He purchased property north of the grand Charles F. Wilcox mansion and commissioned Frank Lobdell (1849-1910) of Lobdell & Mahoney to design his residence. C. F. Scammon, the area's premier builder, received the contract.

Caius Tacitus Ryland came to San Jose with the forty-niners and his law practice prospered. In 1869, he founded the McLaughlin & Ryland Bank and built a magnificent building in San Jose in 1872. In 1874, it became the Commercial & Savings Bank, which was bought by the Bank of Italy in 1910. Caius' wife was the daughter of Peter Burnett, the first governor of California. Their son Joseph followed in his father's footsteps, creating the Commercial Bank of Los Gatos in 1889. The bank, across from the depot about where Le Boulanger is today, burned in the October 1, 1901 fire and its assets were sold. J. R. Ryland went on to the presidency of San Jose Water (1912-1928).

Authentic light fixtures are important to the current owner, such as two pendants from the San Jose Opera House on the porch.

Ryland porch

Ryland Living Room

33 West House

60 Rogers Street
Benjamin W. West, **1928**
Expansion: Martha Matson/Cove Britton, **1991-98**

San Francisco landscape architect Benjamin West designed a small Mediterranean retreat for himself in 1928. His summer villa has been modernized and enlarged to almost 3,000 square feet. The leaded glass picture windows are typical of the current owner's pains to remain in character with the original—the caming pattern of the living and dining rooms was duplicated at no small expense in the new family room and elsewhere.

West dining room (left) and new family room (above).

THE VILLAGE OF LOS GATOS,
just prior to incorporation as a
town, was centered on the 1882
bridge across the creek. The
unpaved road to and from the
bridge was the town's main street.
Wooden sidewalks enabled tourists
to explore from the train depot to
the hotel at Pleasant and East Main
without getting too muddy.

EAST MAIN STREET

From the town's inception until the railroad in 1878, all commercial buildings were built on the east bank of creek—starting with Forbes Mill. The railroad, then the Cannery, and finally the fire of 1891 conspired to move the center of downtown to its present location.

Los Gatos Creek south of the Main Street bridge has always been a lovely spot. Stones from this site were hauled to Forbes Mill on an extension of its railroad spur and used to construct walls on Pennsylvania Avenue and elsewhere. Later, Ed Ditto, born in Alabama in 1877, owned the property. Around 1906, Ditto sold to a San Francisco syndicate which constructed a beautiful home and gardens. As chronicler Dora Rankin reported in her "As It Was" column sixty years later, they intended to operate a brothel. The scheme exposed, the house was sold to William Crim, a prominent realtor from San Francisco, whose son, William, Jr., became an architect and designed both the 1913 Town Hall and the First Church of Christ Scientist (1929) on East Main. Ditto's Lane still exists and leads to a private cluster of four homes.

34 El Gato Penthouse Apartments
22 East Main Street
Gianni Siracusa (developer), **1963-64**

The twin five-story towers of the Penthouse Apartments are the tallest buildings in town. As a result of the town's intent to establish higher density residential properties around town, and to encourage an urban "civic center character" to this neighborhood, developer Gianni Siracusa chose a contemporary design. The town's signature cats were painted on the building in 1997.

60 *Penthouse Apartments*

35 Soda Works Plaza

26 East Main Street
Chris Spaulding, **1997-98**

The Soda Works comprises a new, two-story building designed to fit in aesthetically, as well as two recreated historic structures—the Puccinelli House and the Soda Works. Built on the site of the Los Gatos Hotel and Saloon, a small two-story building destroyed by fire in 1968, the new corner block by developer Dave Flick improved a lot that had been vacant for thirty years.

The Reginald J. Puccinelli house behind the hotel, and the hotel's carriage house, which was converted into the Los Gatos Soda Works bottling plant in the 1920s, were "preserved" by the developer—these two structures were carefully dismantled and rebuilt using as many original materials as possible. The plans carefully worked around the 1910 masonry wall along College Avenue, as well. The total cost of the project is estimated at $3 million.

The site also included the Buffalo Trading Company (34 East Main), the demolition of which caused an outcry from local preservationists. The simple western-style building had evolved from an 1880s-era bathhouse and was deemed not historically significant.

Like the Flick Block across the street, the Soda Works building is an example of "mixed use," with four apartments above three retail stores. "Mixed use was the original American city type, and only in the fifties did it come into vogue that all uses should be separate and everything be segregated," architect Chris Spaulding told the *Weekly Times*. "That's how suburbia was built. And now people are realizing that you can create a city center where people both live and work."

SODA WORKS PLAZA includes a cigar lounge (red building, left), the Tapestry bistro (green building, left), and several stores on Main Street (above).

36 Beckwith Block

HD-76-3

27-35 East Main Street
1893 (1892?)
Renovation: John Lien, **1992**

Nathan Edward Beckwith, one of the petitioners for town incorporation and a member of the committee which set the town's boundaries in 1887, was a real estate and insurance man. Some of his buildings on the north side of East Main were destroyed by fire in July 1891 and, unlike some others, Beckwith learned his lesson and rebuilt in brick.

The building housed the post office in 1894 and was the Rex Hotel for most of the 20th century. In 1980, the Los Gatos Inn bed and breakfast moved in upstairs. Severely damaged in the 1989 earthquake, the structure was strengthened and remodeled with apartments above retail in 1992.

The frieze says 1893, but the building does not seem brand new in an 1892 Admission Day (September 9) photograph in the library collection.

37 Flick Block

37-45 East Main Street
Chris Spaulding, **1996**

Like the Soda Works, the Flick Block is a recent project designed to look old. Both buildings employ unusual details, high-quality materials and amenities such as transoms, turrets and balconies. To avoid monotony, architect Chris Spaulding divided this building's front into three distinct façades, based on commercial buildings from the period found in San Jose.

When developer Dave Flick bought it, the site has been vacant for six years. Built at a cost of $825,000, the building includes two 1,000-square foot apartments on the second floor.

BRICK BUILDINGS mark the site of the July 1891 fire that destroyed three blocks of wooden structures. Development since the 1989 earthquake has aimed to extend the downtown retail and dining ambience to the east.

38 Molly's Paradise Motel
46 East Main Street
1947

Built after World War II and at one time featuring a miniature golf course, Molly's Motel (now the Garden Inn) typifies the "garden court" motor hotel trend of the fifties. Visitors should note the beautiful mosaic tile in the entry.

Local legend claims that after marrying Marilyn Monroe at San Francisco City Hall January 14, 1954, Joe DiMaggio eluded the paparazzi by laying low in Los Gatos on the way to a honeymoon in Mexico. We know that DiMaggio's blue Cadillac convertible with "JOE D" license plates "raced out of San Francisco to avoid pursuing photographers." Perhaps the glamorous couple spent the night at Molly's Paradise Motel before turning up in Paso Robles.

http://www.illusion-art.com

39 *Sieta Punto Uno* (7.1)
49 East Main Street
John Pugh (artist), **1991**

Sieta Punto Uno is a *trompe l'oeil* (French for "fool the eye") painting on the side of the building (actually on removable panels) recalling the destruction wrought by the October 1989 earthquake (which registered 7.1 on the Richter scale). Ironically, although many historic buildings were damaged and the quake crumbled more than a few masonry walls as depicted, the building to which the mural is attached sustained only minor damage.

John Pugh has created both indoor and outdoor murals employing "perspective illusionism" around the world, including San Francisco, Honolulu, Fairbanks, and Taipei. His work in Los Gatos includes interior walls, niches and "illusionary doors and portals" in several private residences. The artist finds that his visual trickery captivates and lures his audience to cross an artistic

IMAGINE A TALL, GOTHIC STEEPLE and it is possible to visualize the 1885 Presbyterian Church, built on land donated by Forbes' Mill co-owner Dr. McMurtry. The steeple was truncated during a 1938 remodel and the building was converted to offices when the congregation moved to Shannon Road in 1953.

Sieta Punto Uno *mural.*

63

Sieta Punto Uno, detail. Even when you can see the seams, it still fools the eye.

threshold and thus seduces them into exploring the concept of a particular piece. Mr. Pugh says that "by creating architectural illusion that integrates both optically and aesthetically with the existing environment, the art transcends the 'separateness' that public art sometimes produces."

"The Pre-Columbian symbols in [*Sieta Punto Uno*] convey an optimistic statement about the future, embracing the concept of growth after pain, rebirth after death," Pugh told the *Weekly Times*' Bob Aldrich. "To me, that's what the rebuilding of Los Gatos is all about."

John Pugh's celebrated work is featured in *Painting the Town: Murals of California* by Robin Dunitz and James Prigoff (ISBN 0–9632862–4–2, 1997).

Ferrari-gazing.

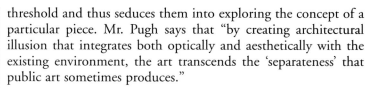

http://www.ferrari-losgatos.com

40 Ferrari of Los Gatos
66 East Main Street

One of Los Gatos' premier tourist attractions, especially after hours, Ferrari of Los Gatos displays fabulous six-figure automobiles, including Rolls Royce, Bentley and Lotus cars, as well as the famed sports cars of Enzo Ferrari (1898-1988). Most evenings, one or two people can be found with their noses pressed figuratively against the glass, often with a bored date left standing on the sidewalk. Presumably, the dealership occasionally sells a car, as well.

There are approximately thirty Ferrari showrooms in the United States, four of them in California. The state and the image go together: one classic Ferrari model is actually named the California. Unless you are closer to Mill Valley or Beverly Hills, you must buy your Ferrari in Los Gatos.

ABOUT 22 PAGEANTS were mounted on the site of the old Co-op Winery. The outdoor stage and scenic backdrop remain as one of the town's most reclusive parks. Crumbling walls from the 1886 winery still retain earth for a parking lot.

Hey, Everybody—Let's Put on a Show

Wilbur Hall must have said words to this effect in 1919, just after The Great War, when Bunker Hill Park became Memorial Park to honor the men killed Over There. Wilbur, a noted Los Gatos author, discussed the idea with poetess Ruth Comfort Mitchell and other artists in his acquaintance.

The location was a challenge: The University Avenue Grammar School was about to be rebuilt and the High School did not yet have an auditorium. The six-year-old Town Hall was not available and the town's Opera House had become Crider's Department Store. These difficulties did not deter the resourceful Hall.

Hall presented his production using local talent outdoors on the grounds of John Cilker's old Co-operative Winery behind Town Hall, which had been mostly torn down five years before. He wrote and directed *Fulfillment*, a modest story of the Earth's creation and man's development, culminating with present day Los Gatos. Billed as the town's "first annual" pageant, the nighttime spectacle used the bluff below Cleland Avenue as a backdrop and concluded a day of picnicking, sporting events, an auto hill-climbing contest on Glen Ridge, and street dancing, on June 21, 1919.

The second annual pageant, *The Californian*, was also a Hall production and this one told a story. Dignitaries attending the two-night performance included Mrs. Fremont Older (wife of the famous San Francisco newspaper editor and aunt to our own columnist John Baggerly) and California Governor William Dennison Stephens, who said afterward that, "As an illustration of history, the pageant was the finest thing I have ever witnessed."

Ruth Comfort Mitchell, Henry Crall and others assisted Hall. In 1920, a group of citizens bought the land, saving it from development. Henry Crall, son of the local stationer, had managed the Opera House before serving in France during the war and he returned filled with ideas. He began building a French Chateau (see 75) and wrote and directed the 1928 pageant, *Tashida*.

Some Pageants & Their Authors

1919	*Fulfillment* (Wilbur Hall)
1920	*The Californian* (Wilbur Hall)
1928	*Tashida* (Henry Crall)
1929	*The Magic Lamp*
1935	*Frontier Days*
1940	*Trail Days* (Owen Atkinson)
1946	*The Cats* (Dean Jennings)
1947	*Dick Wittington's Cat* (Kathleen Norris)

Stones and dirt from the widening of Highway 17 were used to remodel the pageant site in 1939. The expansion which created the Los Gatos Bowl was the vision of W. W. Clark of the Chamber of Commerce, who persuaded George Doeltz, designer of Golden Gate Park, to consult on many features, including two ninety foot (27m) waterfalls. Los Gatos High School students provided the labor and installed colored lighting. The great stage was on two levels: a main stage 90 feet wide by 65 feet deep (27 x 20m), and a lower level 40 feet (12m) deep, big enough for teams of horses, wagon trains of prairie schooners and hundreds of players. More than 2,500 seats were installed and the Bowl was dedicated on August 16, 1940. That year's pageant, Owen Atkinson's *Trail Days*, was in celebration of the new four-lane highway to Santa Cruz.

Pageants resumed after the war, but perhaps the audience was distracted and the quaint historic reenactments weren't the draw they had once been. The last Pageant at the Los Gatos Bowl was held in 1947. Pageant Way (formerly Seanor), off East Main at the library, recalls the glory days. The old road to the Co-op Winery, called Grays Lane and LaMontagne, is now called Fiesta Way, in honor of the *Fiesta de Los Gatos* tradition begun in 1957.

WANT TO SEE INSIDE? The Forbes Mill Annex is now a museum, open 12-4 Wednesday through Sunday (closed holidays).

41 Forbes Mill Annex

HD-73-1

75 Church Street
1880, Mill removed: **1916**

This two-story stone building marks the site of the first commercial structure in Los Gatos, the Santa Rosa Flour Mill, a four-story stone establishment finished in 1854 for James Forbes, who went bankrupt just two years later. The existing structure is an annex, built by the mill's later owners in 1880. The annex has been California Historical Landmark No. 458 since 1950 and was placed on the National Register of Historic Places (78000776) in July 1978.

The mill became the Los Gatos Manufacturing Company in 1863, and a bridge from the top floor connected with other buildings and a general store on East Main Street. At the turn of the century, a freight spur left the railroad line just south of today's Saratoga Road, sliced through the Edelen district and crossed the creek on a wooden trestle north of the mill. The facility was used at various times to manufacture flour, ice, gas and electricity. It produced a peak of 100 barrels of ground flour per day in 1881. In 1916, the 62-year-old building was demolished by its new owner, the Pacific Gas & Electric Company, leaving only the annex. In the 1920s, children helped build a suspension bridge across the creek so that this parcel could be used as a playground for the University Avenue Grammar School (now Old Town). Today's steel pedestrian bridge was part of the freeway construction in 1955, virtually mandated by the suspension bridge. Panels on the bridge were painted by local children of all ages reflecting a Los Gatos heritage theme.

In August 1996, the San Jose University Archaeology Field School, led by Pat Dunning, began excavating at the site of the original mill (southwest of the annex) and discovered square nails, window hardware and other artifacts.

MASONIC HALL, 131 East Main, 1954.

THIRD TIME'S THE CHARM for the oldest denomination in Los Gatos. The First United Methodist Church was established on this site, purchased for $1 gold coin from the owner of Forbes Mill in 1867. The simple original meeting room was replaced by a gothic church, dedicated December 29, 1889 which lasted until 1965. The modern sanctuary shown here was designed by Higgins & Root in 1964.

http://www.gdserv.com/lgfumc

Cost: $806,766, or $23/sq. ft.
*Structural Engineer: Frank E.
McClure & David Messinger.
Mechanical/Electrical Engineer:
Chamberlin & Painter. Landscape
Architect: Sasaki, Walker, Lackey
Assoc., Inc. General Contractor: E.
A. Hathaway & Co.*

http://www.los-gatos.ca.us/los_gatos/los_gatos.html

42 Civic Center
110 East Main Street
Charles D. Stickney & William R. Hull, **1966**

Although the replacement of the 1913 Town Hall was controversial and the town's library now needs larger accommodations, most would agree that the Los Gatos Civic Center exhibits both efficiency and timeless beauty. The design is the result of an architectural competition held in the spring of 1963. The winners were two young architects working in a large Bay Area architectural firm, and they promptly quit to form their own office in Berkeley.

Most of the complex is underground, including the Council Chambers, with a fountain on the roof deck and apparently separate structures for the Town offices, Police and Library. All three are connected at the lower level. Following the urban renewal approach taken by the high school, all other buildings were cleared from the 13-acre site with 500-foot (152 m) frontage on Main to provide a gracious setting for the architecture.

On April 5, 1995, a grand oak tree, which probably bore witness to the granting of the original rancho, suddenly fell, grazing the Police Department building. (A plaque on the tree mentioned Teddy Roosevelt, but he didn't visit Los Gatos on the day in April 1903 that he planted a tree in Campbell.)

The Civic Center lawn is home to the Kiwanis Club's *Fiesta de Artes*, the town's art and wine festival, the third weekend of each August.

A SLOW-CHANGING EXHIBIT of public art graces the civic center lawn. *Eolian* by Eric Ziemelis has been on loan to the town since September 1991. The artist also designs custom furniture (http://www.bzstudios.com).

67

Neighborhood Center

OLD TAMALE, Angelia Lucero, sold hot tamales every day from her red cart until her death February 14, 1902. Her one story Italianate Victorian at 17 Fiesta Way, built circa 1880, was remodeled most recently in June 1998.

Los Gatos High School

43 Neighborhood Center
208 East Main Street
Hedley & Stark Associates, **1978-80**

The two-story, 11,236 sq. ft. brick Downtown Neighborhood Center was built as a senior center. It currently houses the town's Community Services Department and includes meeting rooms used by many different organizations, from the Friends of the Library to Alcoholics Anonymous.

Architect William W. Hedley, Jr., of Campbell, designed the building to incorporate the plain concrete cornice-level banding of the Civic Center as well as to introduce wood and glass elements into the vocabulary. The irregular, cantilevered façade creates more shadow play than the blocky town center across the street.

The town's initial request for bids produced a single bidder at a cost twice Hedley's estimate. The town thereupon acted as its own general contractor, delaying construction, but bringing the project in for $871,000, not including furnishings. After groundbreaking on October 2, 1978, the new facility officially opened March 22, 1980.

44 Los Gatos Union High School
High School Court
William Henry Weeks, Herndon & Finnigan (builder), **1925**

Los Gatos High School was founded in 1887 at the University Avenue Grammar School. Twenty years later, a building program was necessary to accommodate the growing enrollment at both the grammar and high school. A new High School was built on High School Court off East Main Street and dedicated March 10, 1908.

The dramatic classical revival portico, understated decoration and dignified front lawn which we see today was part of a major renovation approved in January 1923 and completed two years later. A music wing was constructed as a WPA project in 1935. The 1925 building hid the 1908 mission-revival structure, which became a wood shop until it was demolished as part of a 1954 development that added the Industrial Arts and Home Economics Buildings, a Boy's Gymnasium and the swimming pool. Coach Douglas White Helm served the school from 1923 until his death in 1953 and the athletic field is named in his honor.

HELM FIELD is named for popular coach Douglas White Helm.

Until Saratoga built its own high school in 1959, Los Gatos Union students came from much farther away. Actress Olivia de Havilland (*Gone with the Wind*), perhaps the most famous LGHS alumnus (1934), came from Saratoga, for example.

Architect William Weeks (1864-1936) designed over 400 schools in Northern California, including the Campbell Union Grammar School (11 East Campbell Avenue) and, with his son, Harold, the Campbell Union High School (1 West Campbell Avenue). Ralph Wyckoff, of the San Jose firm of Wyckoff & White, completed the revised University Grammar School in 1923 and may have participated in the high school design as well.

Home of the Wildcats

Los Gatans are understandably proud of their High School and its standard of excellence. A few years ago, a state survey found that 93% of incoming freshmen intended to go on to college. More impressive, perhaps—84.6% of them actually did.

 45 A Place for Teens
4 New York Avenue
John Lien, **1992-94**

A club for teenagers has existed in the civic center area since the 1930s. In 1941, volunteers built a log cabin where the town offices are today and expanded the Youth Center in 1953. Forbes Mill Annex was a teen center in the early 1970s. But in the mid-1980s, the youth of Los Gatos were again without a place to call their own.

The Outhouse; A Place for Teens

The Outhouse, as the Place for Teens has been known following a community-wide teen contest, opened in September 1994. The vision of Gladie Rabitz, Sue Anawalt, Dru Barth and many others too numerous to name, the project represents the community's generosity. The unusual design of the building was donated

69

by local architect John Lien. The facility offers a safe, supervised, drug-free environment for meetings, concerts, homework, workshops and a computer lab, pool tables and television.

The building is hidden behind the high school, almost up against Highway 17. Teens and visitors are welcome. Boy and Girl Scouts and other local groups use the cabins north of the Outhouse and an unadvertised trail leads south to Forbes Mill.

46 First Church of Christ Scientist
238 East Main Street
William H. Crim, Jr., **1930**

Architect William Crim, Jr. designed the Town Hall in 1913 and walked past it each day as he traveled from his family's home on Dittos Lane (south of the Penthouse Apartments) to the construction site of the First Church of Christ Scientist.

The congregation, which met at 75 Broadway, broke ground for the new church September 1929, one month before the stock market crash which led to the Great Depression. Rushing things a bit, perhaps, the first services were held February 1930.

The building illustrates many aspects of classical, or Greek Revival architecture, from its proportions to its decoration. The columns are a simplified Corinthian order.

First Church of Christ Scientist

47 Hardinge House   HR-12
262 East Main Street
c**1887** Renovation: Britt-Rowe, **1995**

Harley A. Hardinge was an attorney with strongly-held political beliefs that he did not hesitate to share—first with the public, by placing anti-prohibition billboards on his house during the 1905 debates on the subject and later by harassing the town council. The problem with outlawing liquor, he felt, was economic. One photo hanging in the library illustrates the sarcastic tone of his signs: "Wanted: 1600 suckers to buy the vacant property in this rank, rotten, and rusty, dead, dry town before we lose it for taxes…" Another sign read, "Tax rate increased 20%…Hurrah for Prohibition." The town went dry in 1906.

In 1912, lawyer Hardinge vociferously opposed the construction of a Town Hall, which was built anyway the following year. Hardinge lived in this house (with his wife Catherine) as a local, vocal critic until the late 1930s.

LOCAL SINGER DIANE OGILVIE, the developer of this 1995 retail/residential Town Court project expects to build an 83-room hotel next to the Neighborhood Center in 2000.

48 Sunshine Market
308 East Main Street
c1905

James Hicks Pearce (c1850-c1932), scion of the Pearce family (see 90) general store on North Santa Cruz Avenue, struck out on his own and sold groceries here at the east end of Main Street around the turn of century. James and Henrietta Pearce lived in a small house behind the market, and James served on the town council 1902-06.

THREE-TIME OLYMPIC hammer-thrower Ed Burke—and his coach (and wife) Shirley—opened the Los Gatos Athletic Club at 285 East Main in 1981.

http://www.lgac.com

A MARKET FOR 80 YEARS, the Pearce Grocery was converted to other uses c1975 and is now a hair salon.

Development was centered east of the creek, as shown in this 1900 view looking west from the Cypress Way area. The cluster near the center of the photograph is now the High School and Civic Center lawns on East Main Street.

ALPINE & OAK HILL

The foothills east of the creek were originally owned by men like Frank M. Jackson, Samuel Templeton, and Alexander Hildebrand. Jackson, later the postmaster, bought 13 acres in 1883. Templeton was born in Ireland and owned 500 acres in the Santa Cruz Mountains at one time, before building his home in Los Gatos in 1875. German-born Hildebrand practiced architecture in San Francisco 1851-81, before retiring to the 71.25 acres of Oak Hill he purchased in December 1880. Alpine Avenue was reportedly named to attract German tourists from San Francisco to the summer cabins. Upper Alpine was at one time known as Templeton Avenue.

Villa Ceccanti

49 Villa Ceccanti

42 Central Avenue
Quintino Ceccanti, **1906**

Qui Chianti

(Here's wine)

"An evening at Villa Ceccanti was like a visit to Quintino's home..."

Quintino Ceccanti, a native of Tuscany, was one of Los Gatos' most colorful characters. The owner of a successful bohemian restaurant in San Francisco, *Il Ritrovo Sociale* (the social meeting place), he sold everything and moved south after the 1906 earthquake and fire. He rode the trolley to the end of the line and spent time at the El Monte Hotel (Pleasant and East Main) before buying an 1887 house on Oak Hill along with part of A. Hildebrand's 47 acres. Ceccanti began a ceaseless building and tinkering program that ended only when he died in 1936.

An evening at Villa Ceccanti was like a visit to Quintino's home. He was the maitre'd, the chef, the winemaker...as well as the stonemason, carpenter, sculptor, mosaicist, and vineyardist. If he knew you could take a joke, he would ceremoniously weigh you before and after dinner. He was very patriotic—one of his mosaics featured Abraham Lincoln—but he thumbed his nose at Prohibition, which landed him in jail on several occasions. The authorities assumed that his "Qui Chianti" sign referred to his name rather than the literal translation: "Here's wine."

In 1937, Quintino's daughter and son-in-law, Rena and Guilo A. Bocci, reopened the restaurant as the Florentine Village. Business declined in the 1960s, and the facility was converted to apartments in 1972. Today only the rusting sign remains of the restaurant/villa.

50 Sund Farmhouse
107 Foster Road
Herman Sund, **1884**

STEADFAST VALUES helped create Los Gatos and it is fitting that this farmhouse that has been continuously occupied by a member of the Sund family abides, witness to three centuries.

Herman Sund bought a tiny cabin and 30 acres from Peter Johnson in 1882. The cabin may have been the Johnson home in the early 1860s (see 60). Herman (1845-c1922), a ship's carpenter born in northeast Sweden, jumped ship in New York. He married Josephine Peterson in Kansas and came to California for her health. He lost her to tuberculosis in Knight's Ferry and came to Los Gatos with their three children, where he met and married Anna Louisa Schrepfer in 1883. Anna (1858-1943), was the Swiss neice of a Civil War veteran who had retired to the Foster Road area.

Herman improved the cabin in 1884, opened a lumber yard on Johnson Avenue and served on the first town council (1887-1890). As a contractor, he built the Cannery, the Los Gatos Store, several wineries and fruit drying plants and many of the area's finest homes. He built the Keeley Institute on East Main which served as the Town Hall until 1913. He completed many vital civil engineering projects as well, such as street drainage and the town's wooden sidewalks.

LIKE SOME ENDANGERED SPECIES, the stone walls on either side of Alpine Avenue are protected by Historic Designation HD-73-9. The rock was quarried from Los Gatos Creek south of Main Street and is similar to rock found on Pennsylvania Avenue and elsewhere in town.

Herman's son, Russell Henry (1886-1976), was also a builder. In 1907, he built a home at 103 Alpine for his new bride, Margaret Cox. (They later returned to the family farmhouse.) Russell served on the fire brigade, was a Master of the Masonic Lodge in 1914 and served as a member of the board of key institutions such as the electric company (later PG&E) and the Los Gatos Telephone Company. He served on the town council 1932-40 and he built the fire house (78) and the Mail-News Building (11) among many other local projects.

Herman had intended to subdivide his prune and pear orchards in the 1880s, but his vision was delayed until the creation of Sund Avenue in the 1980s. Russell's grandson-in-law, builder Tom Ward, has restored the farm house beautifully.

The original farmhouse, painted sunny yellow, a charming parcel of land and an ancient eucalyptus tree with a 29' (9m) circumference remain as monument to the Sund family's remarkable contribution to our community.

51 Moser House

🔺 HR-8

75 Alpine Avenue
Levi Kimball, **1885**

Built for Levi W. Kimball, this beautiful two-story Victorian was the home of Thomas S. and Esther Moser from 1889 (or earlier) to 1916. Thomas was an English farmer and the couple moved to Los Gatos from Oakland. Sarah Winchester, who began construction of her Mystery House in 1884, was a friend and an occasional visitor.

In the 1920s, another Englishman named Hugh Drury owned the house. Drury was a golfer and was active in the Pebble Beach polo scene. After 1926, Mrs. J. Alfred Powell operated it as a boarding house known as the Alpine Lodge. The current owners received a Bellringer award in 1977 and have lived in the house for over a quarter century.

The hand-turned walnut stair railing sweeps a full 180 degrees. The entry hall is separated by a wall from the servants' stairs which feature triangular treads called winders. Pocket doors with cleverly engineered pulls separate the front and rear parlors. Illustrated tiles surrounding the dining room fireplace inspired several generations of children to make up their own nursery rhymes.

TURNED-WALNUT RAILING must have been wickedly difficult to coerce. The house reportedly cost $8,000 to build—$3,000 of it for the staircase.

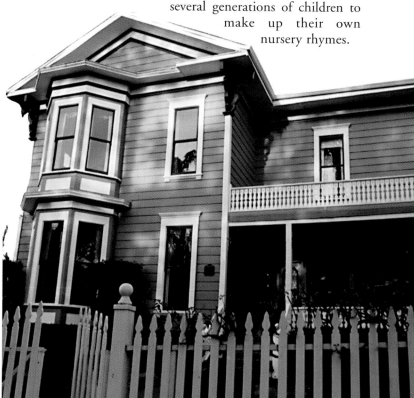

THE ESTHER MOSER HOUSE. The entry features a turned walnut balustrade and provides access to the dining room (top, right) and the living room (left). The long-time current owners have installed a pool and other facilities in the rear, and the porch roof was improved with a balustrade, but the tasteful furnishings and appointments are perfectly in character. Some rooms have been modernized, such as the second-floor office (top, left), but without sacrificing the essence.

Eagle's Nest

52 Eagle's Nest
17681 Foster Road
William May, **1963**

Eagle's Nest is an exuberant expression of 1960s modern style. The house consists of three round pavilions with eleven doors to the outside, nine of them sliding glass. Glass extends from the slab to the flat roof deck with exposed beams, inspiring some to call the house a "round Eichler." (Eichler Homes built many tracts of architect-designed houses featuring slab floors, post and beam structure with exposed wood deck ceilings and sheet glass.) The slab does not include radiant heat (typical of the era) but, otherwise, it's an "All-Electric, Gold Medalion Home," in the General Electric advertising vernacular.

The home was built by Dr. Paul Rosen and his wife Shirley during the construction of Guadalupe College. The land was once owned by Owen Atkinson, a prominent author and newspaperman who wrote the story for the MGM film *20 Mule Team* (1940) and the "Trail Days" 1939 town pageant. Atkinson and his wife called the property "Tilted Acres." In the early 1940s, they rented a house on the property to Northern California's first Guide Dogs for the Blind, which later relocated to San Rafael.

The house was purchased from the Rosen family in 1996 by Alastair and Peggy Dallas. Their name, "Eagle's Nest," derives from an architectural review of the home in the San Francisco *Chronicle* shortly after it was built.

DRAMATIC BUT INCONGRU-OUS, the Fitinghoff House shares its site with the concrete chapel.

53 Guadalupe College
17975 Foster Road
Gaul & Voosen, **1962-64**

Built at a cost of $4 million, including furnishings, by the Sisters of Charity of the Blessed Virgin Mary of Dubuque, Iowa, Guadalupe College was planned to expand the capacity of the order's 130-year-old Mt. Carmel novitiate in Iowa. In February 1968, thirteen women became the first and only class to complete the training, and plans were made to convert the college to use as a cultural or conference center. That plan, as well as a proposal in January 1983 to convert the college into a women's prison, fell to concerted neighborhood opposition, based largely on inadequate roads to the site. Heavily damaged in the 1989 earthquake, the complex has been vacant for almost 30 years.

THE ENTIRE WEST WALL of the chapel is stained glass.

The 57-acre site, purchased from Louis Fitinghoff, included Mr. Fitinghoff's Frank Lloyd Wright-inspired home and extensive prune orchard. The home stayed, but the prunes were replaced by a grand concrete chapel with three stained glass panels facing the setting sun and a complex of three-story residential and classroom wings.

In 1998, after thirty years of senescence, the property was finally sold to a developer who has plans to pulverize and recycle the concrete college on site and create luxury homes, each on multi-acre lots, with the southern portion of the property dedicated to open space.

CONVERTING A CLOISTERED SCHOOL for nuns into a women's prison seemed like a bad idea to area residents in 1983.

ALOOF AND ALONE, an architectural statement by South African designer Stanley Saitowitz is only visible (bottom) from the college.

DORMITORIES AND CLASS-ROOMS were all in place in 1964 for students who never came. The college produced only thirteen graduates.

JOHNSON & CROSS WAY,
named for Anna Cross.

JOHNSON & LOMA ALTA

Johnson Avenue is named for Peter Johnson, a Danish immigrant who provided stable services to the teamsters plying the Santa Cruz Gap Turnpike. On February 7, 1921, the town considered changing the name of the street to El Monte Avenue, but residents objected. Market Street, also named by Mr. Johnson when he subdivided the area in the early 1880s, was changed to reflect the street's residential character. Market became known as Loma Alta (highland) Avenue.

THE MACABEE HOUSE is Eastlake-style, identified by the turned wood columns on the porch and the turned pendants.

54 Macabee Gopher Trap Factory   HD-75-2
110 Loma Alta Avenue
1894

In 1887, Zephyr Macabee (1858-1940) was one of the signers of the petition for town incorporation. His father, Canadian Edward Macabee, owned the El Monte Hotel at East Main and Pleasant Street. The second son of eight children, Zepf came here when he was seven and worked at the El Monte as a clerk, handyman and busboy. He was later a barber for ten years, after which he was advised to work outside for health reasons.

In 1900, he invented the Macabee Gopher Trap, considered a godsend by orchardists in the Santa Clara Valley and worldwide. By the mid-1920s, some 1,000 traps per day were manufactured in this house and the Macabee family's residence had moved to Reservoir Road. In 1955, more than 230,000 traps were produced in this residential factory. For many years, Neta Snook Southern, the author of *I Taught Amelia Earhart to Fly*, assembled traps here. The company still sells traps from this house; stacked boxes waiting for shipment are occasionally visible through the window.

Market Street School

55 Market Street School   🔺 HR-1
179 Loma Alta Avenue
Peter Johnson?, **1891**

Built as a part-residence, part-schoolhouse for first and second graders, the house was apparently originally owned by Peter Johnson, whose daughter, Elvira V. Johnson, taught at the school. Starting in 1894, one room of the house was used as a primary school for the next twenty years. The 1902 directory lists the address as the Eastside School, Miss E. Johnson, teacher. It became a residence again in 1917.

56 Starr House
206 Loma Alta
1893

Built for Mrs. A. J. Starr, who may have been a summer resident, the house was not originally shingled. Chris and Denise Benson (see 17), owners since 1973, remodeled it as a classic Craftsman bungalow of the sort Bernard Maybeck created in the Berkeley hills in the early years of the century. (Maybeck experimented with rich red and blue pigments, too.)

Marcellite Wall and her husband Richard bought the house in 1965. Marcellite had been an artist with Walt Disney Productions and had provided the voice for Minnie Mouse over the years. Ensconced in Los Gatos, she created the Señor Gato cartoon character which appeared in the *Times-Observer* in the 1960s.

206 Loma Alta

206 Loma Alta

http://www.emq.org/confcenter.htm

57 Eastfield Ming Quong
499 Loma Alta Avenue

HR-13

The Spreckles Hospital, a sanitarium on twelve acres at the top of Loma Alta, is now the Los Gatos Conference Center of Eastfield Ming Quong. Ming Quong, an organization founded in 1915 to care for Chinese orphans, acquired the property in 1936. Ming Quong means "radiant light," and they gratefully named the Spreckles house "Sunshine Cottage." In 1987, Ming Quong merged with San Jose's first orphanage, the Home of Benevolence (founded 1877), which changed its name in 1951 to, simply, Eastfield.

MOVED FROM MAIN STREET, a site across from the high school, in 1952, the house at 5 Spring Street earned a Bellringer award in 1987. "Once you add a second floor, you've lost the original house," says Michael Krolak, who worked with architect Dennis Burrow in 1990 to build a new first floor under the 1890s-era home.

79

A RARE HYBRID of Victorian and Craftsman, the house at 142 Johnson was built in 1888 by Charles H. Wheeler, a builder in competition with Herman Sund.

THE TURNED WOOD post at the porch identifies an example of Eastlake style at 143 Johnson.

PREDATING MORE ELABORATE Queen Anne "cottages," the vernacular Victorian style was often inspired by pattern books of midwest farm house designs. 122 Johnson is a fine example.

200 Johnson

58 Johnson Barn

200 Johnson Avenue
Peter Johnson, **c1880**

Peter Johnson built a barn on this site shortly before creating Johnson Avenue. Two large tanks in back held water used to palliate the dust on the street.

The Reverend William Henry Johnston (a Methodist minister not known to practice) operated a grocery store here from 1903 to 1925 and had the big tanks removed as a safety hazard. The store joined Herman Sund's lumber yard at Johnson and Cross Way, a taxi service at 145 Johnson and a French Laundry at 209 in creating a tiny commercial district.

59 Lyon House
239 Johnson Avenue
1890 Renovation: **1995-**

An Italianate Victorian, identified by its tall windows and prominent cornice, this house also features extremely high ceilings. Jim and Brenda Lyon have been renovating the house since 1995. Born and raised in Los Gatos, Jim serves on the Historic Preservation Committee and is working hard to restore the home accurately. The first step involved raising the two-story home and casting a concrete foundation underneath. Second was restoring an authentic color scheme—the exterior had been painted yellow for many years. An accurate shade of green was finally located in Greenfield Village, Michigan, a museum of the late 19th century created by Henry Ford.

A BIRTHING HOUSE, home of a midwife, for much of this century, according to Jim Lyon, who is assembling a record of the many people born in his home.

1995-2005
RENOVATED BY
BRENDA & JIM LYON
WITH THE HELP AND SUPPORT
OF THEIR FAMILY & FRIENDS

341 Johnson

A STUCCO BOX WITH ALUMINUM WINDOWS at 341 Johnson, built in 1960 (twin to 345), became a Craftsman bungalow in 1992. Architect Peggy Dallas was inspired by Bernard Maybeck's Culbertson House, but also added her own nuanced details. She deliberately turned the entry turret 11 degrees, for example, and filled the resulting gap with glass block. The stained glass in the front door (and elsewhere in the house) was designed and executed by the architect. In place of enclosed down-spouts, an unusual half-round copper gutter leads to heavy chains which direct the water to the ground.

NO NONSENSE VICTORIANS are found in abundance on Johnson Avenue, such as the 1895 Morton House at 348. Note the traditional pyramidal hip roof (behind the gables).

SAN JOSE ROAD

In 1880, properties with frontage on San Jose Road (now Los Gatos Boulevard) extended all the way down to the east bank of the Los Gatos Creek. Farm houses were built on the high ground near the road and the creek-level portion (the "bottom land") was farmed or planted in trees. The bluff overlooking East Main Street was known as El Monte Hill.

Bella Vista dates to 1912 or so, about the time that Glen Ridge came into fashion. The name means "beautiful view."

Peter Johnson

60 Johnson House   HD-73-5
49 Los Gatos Boulevard
Peter Johnson, c**1864**

Peter Johnson (1842-c1897), a Danish immigrant, arrived in this county in 1861 and owned 131 acres on the high ground (El Monte Hill) overlooking East Main Street. No one knows precisely when he and his wife Annie M. Hays (1852-c1927) built this house (perhaps as early as 1864). He kept a barn and black-smith shop across the San Jose Road (Los Gatos Boulevard) from the house. He fathered eight children, subdivided his property, published the Los Gatos *Mail* and served on the town council from 1888 to 1894, the last two years as the equivalent of Mayor.

Stacia Street is named for one of his daughters (we speculate that Miss A. S. Johnson in the town directory might be Annie Stacia). After his death, Annie became a partner in Thomas E. Johns' Rankin Block drug store, creating the Johns & Johnson pharmacy.

The house has apparently had only three subsequent owners, the most recent of whom is renovating with attention paid to historical accuracy.

The huge Coast Live Oak in the front yard is said to predate the house.

83

A MODERN QUEEN ANNE, at 101 Stacia Street. Built new in 1993, it was designed by Michael McKay.

61 Hunter House

46 Los Gatos Boulevard
c**1888** Renovation: Gary Schloh, 1989-90

Built around the time of the town's incorporation for Thomas and Emily Hunter, the house facing Peter Johnson's farm house is Stick Victorian, featuring late-Italianate details such as the porch roof, tall windows and important cornice, but on an asymmetrical facade with a corner bay window.

A tiny sign on the gate to the right reads, "Attention: Chien Bizzarre." The current owners bought the "mad dog" sign in a Paris shop specializing in tin signs.

54 Los Gatos Boulevard

62 Fontaine House

54 Los Gatos Boulevard
1898-1903

Lillian Fontaine (1886-1975) lived in this grand Craftsman house in the 1950s and 1960s and attracted many famous visitors. The mother of actresses Joan Fontaine and Olivia de Havilland was active with the Los Gatos High School drama department. Gracie Allen and George Burns may have been regular visitors.

Built as a summer house for Clara G. Burke, a full renovation was completed just in time for the 1989 earthquake, which caused extensive damage. At great cost, the house was renovated for a second time in 1990-91.

63 I. D. Mabie House
112 Los Gatos Boulevard
c**1920**

Mabie chalet

Irving and Lura Mabie lived in this charming cottage, which has not yet been magnified into a "restored" mansion like so many others in our affluent town. Irving was a Vice President of the Bank of Los Gatos and served on the town council for twenty years (1918-38), including two terms as mayor (1924-26 and 1930-32).

The house offers an excellent example of the stylistic adaptation common during architectural transitions. While it is not a grand Craftsman bungalow, it does not match the modest homes of the 1920s and 1930s either. The front-facing gable, cutout stencil railing and flower boxes at the windows suggest that this house wants to be a Swiss chalet.

COUSIN TO THE SPRECKLES house, 116 Los Gatos Boulevard has similar Eastlake details and may have been the Spreckles' carriage house.

64 Spreckles House
122 Los Gatos Boulevard
Julia & Wm. Alexander (developers), c**1895**

HP-5

After losing their San Francisco home in the great earthquake and fire, Richard and Anne Spreckles bought this home on four acres at Stacia and San Jose Avenue in 1906, in order to raise their children in "the country." Related to sugar baron Claus Spreckels just distantly enough to spell the name differently, Richard was the founding president of the Los Gatos Commuter's Club, organized in March 1912. Note the battered (sloping) wall at both the porch and the base of the house and the turned Eastlake-style porch columns.

Richard later developed the end of Loma Alta Avenue (see 57).

Cohen House

65 Miss Emily Cohen House

HD-76-9

204 Los Gatos Boulevard
Eben W. French (builder), **1892**

Miss Emily L. Cohen (Pettis) was an early organizer and first Secretary-Treasurer of the History Club at the turn of the century. She was the club's long-standing president (1907-1932) and passed away in 1936. Rather than collecting town history, the History Club was formed to study world affairs and culture. The town's Christmas tree, a deodar cedar planted by the club in 1923, is still standing in the town plaza. The organization's 1958 clubhouse stands across the street and is available for weddings and other events.

Simons House

66 Simons House

207 Los Gatos Boulevard
c1889

Daniel Page Simons (1839-1910) was a town trustee (councilman) in 1892-96 and again 1906-1910, the last two years as chairman (mayor). He is listed as a "timber contractor" in one town directory, a "capitalist" in another. His was a strong voice for prohibiting liquor sales in town which led to town voters choosing the so-called "local option" in 1906. Los Gatos was thus the second city in California (after Palo Alto) to go "dry."

67 Whitney House

214 Los Gatos Boulevard
1892

There is no better example in the area of the Victorian "Stick" style than Elijah S. Whitney's stately home. Whitney owned thirteen acres on the east side of San Jose Road which was developed and parlayed by William G. and Julia (Collester) Alexander. The style dates to the middle of the Victorian period (in Los Gatos, 1885-1893, approximately), and is characterized by squared windows and geometric decoration.

68 Vineland School
269 Los Gatos Boulevard
c**1890**, Relocated: **1905**

The Vineland School district joined with Los Gatos in 1905 and this schoolhouse was moved from Farley Road (approximately where today's Jehovah's Witness Kingdom Hall is located) in 1906.

Vineland school

69 Schomberg Piano Factory
256 Los Gatos Boulevard
Julia & Wm. Alexander (developers), **1887**

It may not look like a piano factory, but like Zepf Macabee, Henry Schomberg and his family built pianos on the ground floor of the Mullins House. The family's musical craftsmanship won a ribbon in Chicago (perhaps at the World Columbian Exposition in 1893). Mr. Schomberg served on the town council (1894-98), the last two years as the equivalent of mayor. Notice the carved lyre in the right-hand gable.

GRANDPA RAISED PIGEONS.
The house at 50 Whitney belonged at one time to Jim Hubbel, grandson of Dr. George M. Hubbel, who raised his breed of White King pigeons in town, first on North Santa Cruz Avenue, then, after 1920, on University Avenue. Squab (pigeon) may be the other white meat, but Hubbel's largest market was providing stuffed pigeons with snowy feathers for floral decorations.

87

MULTIMEDIA IN LOS GATOS: The Whitlock Studio, the first radio station in the area, promoted A. A. Whitlock as the "Voice of the Santa Cruz Mountains," and invited local talent to perform (without compensation) in 1927. The house at 271 Los Gatos Boulevard appears to have been the point of emanation.

LAVENDER QUEEN ANNE at 227 Los Gatos Boulevard was largely imagined after the 1989 earthquake, but it is enjoyable to look at with its typically Queen Anne asymmetry and exuberance. The house reportedly sports a five-figure paint job.

A DUSTY SCAR in 1955, when the 17/9 cloverleaf was built, is now a green oasis, especially as viewed from the Bella Vista bridge. The bridge, and the so-called Charles Street extension, were supported by the expansion-minded town council, but not by the voters. For a time, it looked as if the new freeway would not connect with the east half of town. In 1957, the electorate reversed itself and funded construction of the bridge, allowing freeway traffic to reach Los Gatos Boulevard after all.

A BOSTONIAN ON BELLA VISTA, the home at 200 Bella Vista, remodeled by architect Chris Spaulding in 1993, elevates the already dignified avenue.

88

CLASSIC CRAFTSMAN bunga-
low at 402 Bella Vista.

THAT QUIET BELLA VISTA DIGNITY is in evidence in this 1990s
residence at 400 Bella Vista Avenue by architect John Lien.

70 Bartlett House
212 Bella Vista Avenue
Backus Bartlett, **1886**

In 1876, John Goldsworthy owned a swath of land, 130 acres in
all, including this property and the present high school athletic
field and Los Gatos Lodge. (Miss Lily Goldsworthy was a com-
positor on the town's first newspaper in 1881.)
Goldsworthy sold 22.5 acres to Backus L. Bartlett,
the adjuster to the San Francisco Board of Trade, in
1882. There may have been a structure here before,
but Bartlett created his home and began paying
taxes in 1887. In that year, his 400 apricot trees
yielded $175 per acre. Access to the house may have
been from San Jose Road (Los Gatos Boulevard),
but it seems unlikely that the house was rotated to
face Bella Vista as has been suggested.

The house stayed in the Bartlett family until 1914.
Bella Vista was further subdivided in response to
the popularity of Glen Ridge in the 1920s. It is currently the home of Mayor Jan Hutchins and his
wife Teri Hope, who founded the Los Gatos Coffee
Roasting Company (see 20) in 1982. The couple
opened their home for the annual Garden Tour in
1997. Avid gardeners, their rose garden includes
some thirty varieties, some of which were gifts from
Jan during their courtship.

Bartlett House 89

THE WELL-KNOWN CRIDER
mansion was actually built by businessman E. R. Strome of North
Dakota in 1908. The Criders
moved here in 1920 (see 104).

5 Walk to Town

THE QUAINT NEIGHBORHOODS immediately surrounding downtown are known locally by the realtor's sobriquet "Walk to Town." Tidy neighborhoods like Almond Grove, Fairview, and Edelen are right next door to shops and services, suggesting a stroll for some ice cream or just to enjoy the fresh air and people watching.

Broadway was one of the first subdivisions, followed quickly by Edelen at a time when "downtown" was centered on the length of Main Street and access to the depot determined commercial rents. Edelen was the neighborhood closest to the school. The Almond Grove, northwest of the train station behind the Cannery, was somewhat off the beaten path. In the first decades of the twentieth century, North Santa Cruz Avenue, with its electric interurban line, was developed commercially and Almond Grove became more convenient to shopping.

The foothills west of town, though not easy walking distance, are described in this chapter as well, in the Glen Ridge and Overlook & Monte Sereno sections. In 1957, residents of western Los Gatos voted to incorporate rather than be swallowed by the growing town of Los Gatos. Led by a group of retired admirals, the voters created strictly residential Monte Sereno, which takes its name from El Sereno mountain.

The chapter concludes with the Edelen district, which has a subtly different feeling from its cousin the Almond Grove. The town's corporation yard, created by the taming of the creek, lies hidden in Edelen as well.

CONTENTS

SMALL LOTS and white pickets define the quaint neighborhoods closest to town.

91

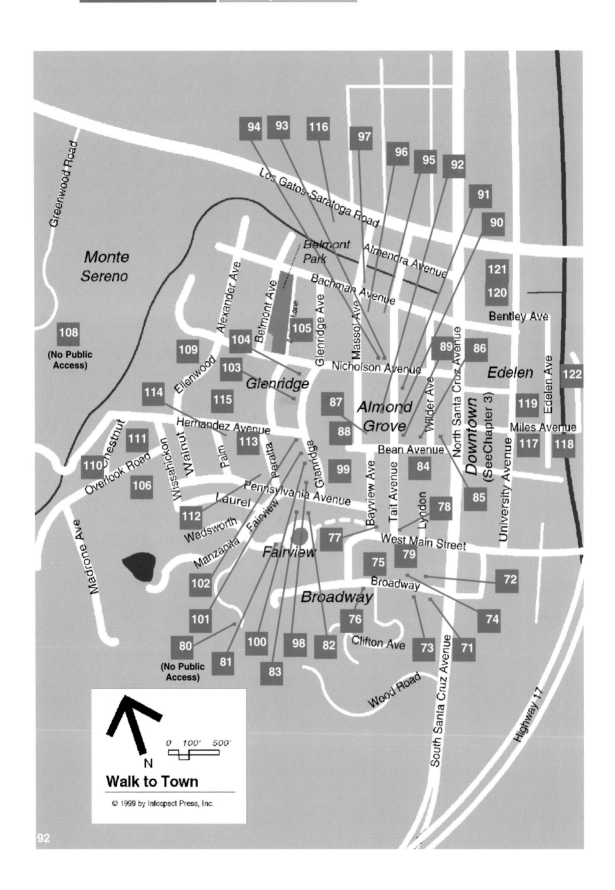

Monte
Sereno

Greenwood Road

Los Gatos-Saratoga Road

94 93 116 97 96 95 92

91

90

Belmont
Park

Almendra Avenue

121
120

Bachman Avenue

Bentley Ave

108
(No Public
Access)

Alexander Ave

Belmont Ave

Ann Lane

105

Glenridge Ave

Massol Ave

Nicholson Avenue

89 86

Edelen

122

109

104

103

Glenridge

Ellenwood

115

87

Almond
Grove

North Santa Cruz Avenue

Wilder Ave

119

Edelen Ave

Miles Avenue

114

Hernandez Avenue

113

88

Bean Avenue

117 118

Downtown
(See Chapter 3)

Chestnut

111

Wissahickon

Walnut

Palm

Peralta

Glenridge

99

Bayview Ave

Tait Avenue

84

University Avenue

110 Overlook Road

106

Pennsylvania Avenue

Lyndon

78

85

112

Laurel

Wadsworth

Fairview

Manzanita

Fairview

77

West Main Street

79

Madrone Ave

102

Broadway

75

Broadway

72

101

76

74

80

100 98 82

Clifton Ave

73 71

(No Public
Access)

81

83

Wood Road

South Santa Cruz Avenue

Highway 17

N

0   100'   500'

Walk to Town

© 1999 by Infospect Press, Inc.

BROADWAY & WEST MAIN

The first developer to subdivide in town was John Weldon Lyndon. As the train reached Los Gatos in 1878, he moved his hotel to the location of today's Lyndon Plaza. As part of Lyndon's expansion, the Ten Mile House became the Los Gatos Hotel, and he created Broadway, a slowly rising road, straight into the hills, with forty-eight house-sized lots which were first offered for sale in September 1881. The lots sold slowly at first, but the location has always been first-class. Lyndon formally dedicated the street on January 5, 1883, four and a half years before the town was incorporated. There are twelve pre-1900 homes remaining.

STAIRS TO THE FRONT DOOR, common at the west end of Broadway, are part of living in this recent example of an in-character remodel by prolific architect Chris Spaulding (1994).

The gentle slope to the south nearest the train station was the tranquil Los Gatos Meadow, where Lyndon later built his mansion and which is now The Meadows retirement home. The south side at the far end of Broadway was called Clifton Mound, where developer Thomas Hayselden built cottages after the town incorporated. Two homes on Clifton Avenue burned when a brush fire approached the town from the south in August 1997. The Abbey Inn, a complex of several buildings on two and a half acres at the end of West Main, was replaced by apartments in the 1980s. Once known as the Riddle Estate, it became a boarding house when Frances Abbey Puckett acquired it after 1922. Joan Fontaine and her sister Olivia de Havilland were residents at one time. In later years, rumors suggest it may have been used as a bordello, likely without the knowledge of the owner. The arrogant demolition of the historic estate in the 1970s spurred enactment of the town's historic preservation codes.

Folk-Italianate at 84 Broadway (above). Compare with 17 Fiesta, page 68). House at 107 Broadway (below) won a Bellringer in 1976.

Even today, Main Street loses steam when it reaches Santa Cruz Avenue. In the nineteenth century, the trail west led up today's Turnstile Walk, over the rise that is now Fairview Plaza and straight up the hill to the estate of Daniel Van Denburg. The continuation of Main past Santa Cruz Avenue was sometimes called Hotel Street. Lyndon's lands extended a block north of Main and lots he sold on Bayview, Montgomery (now Tait) and Lyndon Avenue were presumably less expensive than his premier Broadway.

37 Broadway

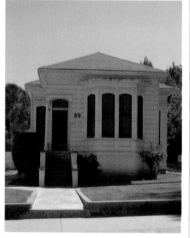

29 Broadway

71 Beckwith House   🔔 HR-9
37 Broadway
Mr. Hudson (builder), c**1890** John Lien, **1994**

The modest home of grocer Harry S. Beckwith has been expanded to nearly four times its original size over the years. The second floor was added in 1896, shortly after Beckwith purchased the home from its original owner, a Mr. Hudson. A "mother-in-law" apartment was added in 1940 and the size ballooned in the 1980s and 90s. Typical of the decade, some of the 1980s-era work was "too modern," and the current owners had to replace well-intentioned remodeling with more authentic appointments.

Harry was probably related to town father Nathan Beckwith, builder of the brick Beckwith Block on East Main Street after the fire of 1891. Harry's grocery, however, was in the Hofstra Block on North Santa Cruz Avenue.

In 1925, this house was home to Lyman L. Feathers of the Star Taxi Company. Lyman was later a traffic officer and during the Great Depression, he made the town jail available to transients—stories abound of the "Feathers Hotel." Feathers was Chief of Police (1939-43) before resigning to return to the taxi business.

As you enjoy the home's beautiful garden from the sidewalk, notice the small house to the left at 29—it has been suggested that it may be an unmodified twin of the original Beckwith House.

72 Farley House
44 Broadway
1890

Home to several generations of public servants, and others, this unusual Greek Revival cottage was built by Judge Ebenezer Clinton Farley (1844-c1920) and his wife Ettie. Eben, as he was called, was a civil war veteran and owner of 18 acres in the Vineland district north of town, where he left his name on Farley Road. This was also the home of E. E. Briggs, postmaster 1950-1966 (see "The Broken Time Machine," page 100).

73 Waterman House 🔔 HR-3
45 Broadway
c1875

A prototypical example of an Italianate Victorian home, the John B. Waterman House defies precise dating. The county assessor's record indicates 1875, and renovation uncovered latches stamped 1866 and a picture in the home's library dated 1870. Further, Italianate styling, with its tall windows, shallow roof and emphasized cornice, was popular early in the Victorian era, only to be eclipsed by the Queen Anne style's porches and turrets in the 1880s and 90s. Nonetheless, some historians date the house only to the 1880s, perhaps because the street had not been sub-divided in the 1870s.

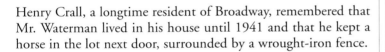

Henry Crall, a longtime resident of Broadway, remembered that Mr. Waterman lived in his house until 1941 and that he kept a horse in the lot next door, surrounded by a wrought-iron fence.

The current owner has been perfecting this lovely mansion for almost thirty years. The stained glass window, for example, is not original. It was found on a church in Santa Clara. In the 1960s, part of the house was an art gallery, entered from the rear.

74 Switzer House
62 Broadway
1885 Restored: **1992**

An example of a Greek Revival style called "four square," this cottage was built by realtor and retired Methodist pastor Wesley Peck. The porch was added in 1910. Lovingly restored by Stan and Lucille Switzer in 1992, it has been home to Harry Ford (of Ford Brothers Cleaners on North Santa Cruz Avenue) in the 1920s, and gopher trap scion Raymond Macabee in the 1970s.

LES MOINEAUX, The Sparrows, Henry C. Crall's life-long labor of love.

75 Chateau Crall
68 Broadway
1919

Henry Christian Crall (1893-1978) was born in Los Gatos and helped in his father's store and Ford's Opera House before going "Over There" in the Great War (World War I). The 25-year-old fell in love with the architecture of the French provinces and began building this Norman villa when he returned in 1919. The five bedroom house required 9,000 bricks and 30 years of love to create—Henry scavenged and acquired materials from all over town. Crall served his community as few have before or since. A 33rd-degree Mason, he was President of the Rotary, a member of the Planning Commission for four years, was appointed to the town council in 1961 and won re-election (1962-66).

Crall's father, Henry Jewett Crall, came to Los Gatos for a visit in 1890 and ended up staying to open "Crall's Palace of Sweets" at 120 West Main. The fire of 1901, which destroyed the store, allowed him to re-think his product line. He reopened as "Crall's Stationery," which later moved to 21 North Santa Cruz and existed until 1981. (H. C. recalled that 21 was the extreme north end of the business district on North Santa Cruz at the time.) The family lived at 66-72 Broadway from the turn of the century.

Crall's Stationery was a four-generation family business, founded by Henry J., then operated by Henry C. and later his son, Henry Lehman, and grandsons Henry Christopher and Craig William. H. L.'s wife Jole was forced to sell the house in 1984 after her petition to operate it as a bed and breakfast was denied.

The house originally had an entrance on West Main Street, but the current owners sold the back parcels and installed a pool.

With a full basement and two stories, the house is now 3,900 sq. ft. Except the kitchen and the family room, every room is on a different level. The spiral stair in the entry turret fell in the earthquake and was replaced by a conventional stair elsewhere, but, in general, the solidly-built home survived the quake quite well.

CRALL'S PALACE OF SWEETS, H. J. Crall, proprietor.

FRENCH HARDWARE on the windows, carved wood mantels in the children's bedrooms, and "Sleep Well" inlaid in the hardwood floor.

CLIFTON WAY GETS RURAL quickly one block south of Broadway. A brush fire in August 1997 damaged several homes here.

76 Hayselden Cottages
89 Broadway
1887

Developer Thomas Hayselden completed this matching set of four cottages (81, 85, 89, 93) within weeks of the town's incorporation. The four houses are built of solid redwood. Town chronicler Bob Aldrich discovered that Bessie Maddern, author Jack London's first wife, lived in one around the turn of the century. Oakland-born London lived near Los Gatos-Almaden Road and Union Avenue at the turn of the century with another woman and visited a friend's ranch in the Santa Cruz mountains known as *Call of the Wild*.

Jack London's daughter Becky fell off this stone wall while playing "horse" in 1907 and cut her five-year-old chin. She was surprised recently to discover that the wall had survived the century along with her.

AS BROADWAY CLIMBS into the hills, it becomes a narrow lane called Broadway Extension. Homes here, including several pre-1900 Bellringers, sit above the road with carriage houses cut into the hillside.

77 Dr. Rice House
312 West Main Street
c**1888** Renovation: Tom Ward (builder), **1970**

Dr. John A. Rice, one of the first dentists in town, purchased this house with his wife Kittie about 1896. The residence, which features a hidden garage door on the Bayview side, was substantially renovated in 1970—the house was raised and a new half-basement built—reportedly including front porch balustrades salvaged from the Lyndon Hotel. Note the square, not round, turret.

78 Los Gatos Museum

4 Tait Avenue
Maurice C. Couchot, Jesse Rosenwald, **1927**

THE LOS GATOS MUSEUM is open 12-4, Wed.-Sun.

Before building this Spanish-revival firehouse, completed in July 1927, Los Gatos employed equipment sheds at both ends of town for use by the all-volunteer force. Herman Sund built this and the Mail-News building (see 11) in the late 1920s. This structure contained the fire chief's office and protected the La France pumping engine, which is possibly the same engine enjoyed by children today at Oak Meadow park.

Left unused after Los Gatos joined the Central Fire Protection District, the firehouse opened as a museum May 20, 1967. Most town history archives are kept at Forbes Mill, while the Tait facility focuses on culture and art. Don't overlook the peaceful, shady resting area next to the museum on West Main Street.

Gem City

Automobile Garage

Renting

Storage   Repairing

—Early service station on West Main near Lyndon, 1907.

79 Trailer House

249 West Main Street
c**1888**

Nearly forgotten by recent historians, Lewis C. Trailer was an early realtor and insurance agent with offices in the Parr Block, 140 West Main (now the Opera House). A director of the Commercial Bank, he was a candidate for Town Treasurer in 1894, but lost to fellow banker J. J. Stanfield. This dignified Victorian may have been the Trailer home, though town directories of the period list his address as simply "West Main." Notice the exposed plumbing outside the west wall.

99

The Broken Time Machine

Who cared if the dial was stuck, the thing was working! It was miraculous...the time machine was allowing me to listen to the sounds of Fairview Plaza as if I were there. I heard children playing outside—children who by now would be well started on careers. I was tuned in to Thursday, May 7, 1981 at about 7:30 in the evening. People were talking and they had not met before so, luckily for me, they introduced themselves.

Ron Bender, a well-spoken high school teacher and then the proud owner of a Fairview home, was receiving Irma and Ed Briggs who had been married in Ron's living room over fifty years before when the house was only forty years old. Clear as a bell, I could hear them discussing cats and how late the grocery store stayed open. Before Irma's family moved in, the house had different owners—the Doolans. Ed remembered playing with their son in 1906 or so. "They were well-to-do," Ed said. Their son had electric toys. Irma recalled that this same family left a trunk in the basement in which she found a beautiful Victorian dress when her family bought the house. Ed spoke of delivering groceries from his father's store by bicycle. Many of the homes on the plaza were rented for the summer by people from San Francisco, Irma remembered.

The voices faded. The Briggs were saying goodbye. I twisted the dial urgently, but my portal to 1981 closed. Paper records and old photographs are not the only ways to capture the past, it turns out. A simple tape recorder can be a conduit connecting generations.

FAIRVIEW PLAZA

If the term gracious defines a combination of dignity and accessibility, Fairview Plaza qualifies. Only about 20 homes surround a tiny park, with an unmarked, ten foot wide pedestrian shortcut called Turnstile Walk leading to town.

Frank McCullagh subdivided Fairview in the mid 1880s, after Broadway but before Almond Grove. Perhaps inspired by Riverside, an influential tract outside Chicago designed by Frederick Law Olmstead and Calvert Vaux in 1869, McCullagh's streets curved and provision was made for common greenspace. A native of Philadelphia, he created Pennsylvania Avenue and a switchback to high ground above the end of West Main Street. There were 28 original lots. Twelve homes were built by 1900, a total of 19 by 1925.

The Campfire Girls created a bird sanctuary and fish pond in Fairview Park in 1927, but the simple benches and planted islands one sees today were installed in 1962. In the late sixties, the plaza was reportedly "hippieville," filled with funky cars, music and marijuana.

91, 95 Fairview

ONE HORSE BARN not yet converted to house automobiles, the whitewashed structure behind 57 Fairview seems to expect its original owner, retired pastor Rev. Wesley Peck's buggy to return from town any day now.

SOMETHING NAUTICAL LURKS just beyond description in John E. Ellis' 1886 home at 78 Fairview.

Fairview Park

101

Perkins House gates

DAYLIGHT POKES THROUGH to the attic of Maria Bendroit's 1898 cottage at the east end of the Plaza, the victim of flying embers from the August 1997 brush fire. Scaffolding-like sticks are "story poles" which show the extent of proposed remodeling and expansion.

80 Clara Huntington Perkins House
40 Fairview Plaza
Julia Morgan, **1919**

Clara Huntington Perkins, the adopted daughter doted on by railroad magnate Collis P. Huntington, was an artist and sculptor who considered architect Julia Morgan a friend. Clara was, by 1919, divorced from Mr. Perkins, described as a "fortune-hunting German prince." She commissioned Morgan to design a fabulous estate for her in the untrodden hills of the extreme South Bay.

Eight years before beginning work on San Simeon for William Randolph Hearst (and four years after designing the Saratoga Foothill Women's Club), Julia Morgan designed a Mediterranean hilltop villa for Clara that cost $90,000 to build. The long driveway winds up and up, creating a sense of mystery about the house before one even reaches the columned loggia that leads to the front door. A long hallway connects the two wings of the 5,000 square foot, single-story residence. All ten rooms feature wide-plank teak floors and each major room opens to the outdoors. Morgan gave the living room a sixteen foot (5m) ceiling. For her part, Clara went shopping in Italy and returned with a Carrera marble fireplace and a full teak ceiling for the living room.

Educated at the University of California at Berkeley and the *Ecole des Beaux Arts* in France, and occasionally mentored by Bernard Maybeck, the diminutive (five foot, 1.5m) Morgan began her career in the Bay Area shortly before the San Francisco earthquake. She is considered one of the great architects of the 20th century, but when she retired in 1951, with few clients asking for her kind of work anymore, she destroyed all her drawings and office records.

Two families live on the property today, one in the Perkins house and one in the large Julia Morgan-designed guest house. Clara Perkins described Morgan's design as a typical "renaissance hillside retreat for a former princess seeking privacy," and the current owners of the Perkins House are likewise reclusive. The only part of the estate visible from the public right of way is the two gateposts at the end of the winding private drive.

Scammon House

68 Fairview Plaza
C. F. Scammon (builder), **c1885**

Scammon House

Possibly the first home in Fairview Plaza, this house was built before 1886 by builder Charles F. Scammon for himself. Mr. Scammon, President of the Los Gatos Real Estate and Building Association, built many of the fine homes in town, including the Malpas House (55 Hernandez, see 114), the Parr House, the Bean-Gober residence at North Santa Cruz and Bean Avenue (demolished in 1938), and the Urquhart House at 19 Glenridge (98). By 1897, Mrs. Sarah M. Place owned the house. Sarah was the widow of undertaker Alexander Place and mother of Elvert, who carried on the family business and would later convert the Coggeshall Mansion into a funeral parlor.

The house has been divided in recent years, and person-high fences likewise apportion the front yard with three numbered gates to the street. Gate number three leads to a narrow fenced walkway and a rear door.

82 Barngrover House

91 Fairview Plaza
c1901

BOOHER HOUSE at 90 Fairview Plaza belongs with the plaque at the east end of the tiny park. Miss Margaret Booher lived here for more than 40 years. Victor Booher, her brother, Los Gatos High School class of 1931, known as "Mr. Clean" to many, is remembered as a thin, frail man who swept downtown sidewalks.

Harvey M. Barngrover, like John Bean, sold orchard equipment. Beginning with Luther Cunningham's patented prune dipper, the Anderson-Barngrover firm of San Jose quickly built a broad line of fruit processing machinery. After competing for nearly three decades, the company merged with its next-door neighbor, the Bean Spray Pump Company, to form the Food Machinery Corporation, today the conglomerate known as FMC.

Mr. Barngrover built his house comparatively late, probably after the turn of the century. It is a nicely restored example (like 54 Los Gatos Boulevard, 62) of Free Classical style, a simplification of both Queen Anne and Greek Revival concepts. The three-part window facing the street is called a Palladian window, after Renaissance architect Andrea Palladio.

Barngrover House

103

FROG HOLLOW derives from the owner's nickname, Frog. The apartment upstairs is "Up Frog Hollow."

83 Frog Hollow
89 Fairview Plaza
1892

Mr. F. N. Smith, possibly the Southern Pacific stationmaster, built this house on land bought from Frank McCullagh in 1892, using plans bought from the Sears catalog. At one point it was a boarding house for lumbermen, and evidence in the walls suggests that the 1890s version of a hot plate caused a fire at one time.

The home's most notorious resident, R. P. Doolan, arrived from San Francisco in 1906 and spent money liberally in an effort to win election to the equivalent of the town council. He succeeded in 1910, after a contested ballot count, and apparently, his prize won, became bored. Without selling this house, he returned to San Francisco and missed many council meetings. In cahoots with councilman George Turner, Doolan's minority was able to keep the council from accomplishing anything on several occasions. In March 1913, the council resolved that he should resign, but he resisted and served out his term.

The current owner tells of observing a man in his eighties standing in Fairview Park looking at her house. He explained that the upstairs front bedroom had been his when he was eight. Tending an old house requires love, and the owner, like so many other Los Gatans, is a fine caretaker. It creaks and groans, she says, and "every once in while, the house takes a deep breath."

GONZO SLEPT HERE. Dave Goelz, the puppeteer who performs and gives voice to Gonzo the Great, Waldorf and other Muppet characters lived in this 1893 house from 1970 to 1973. Goelz has been with the Muppet troupe since 1973 and is credited with the 1976 television program and several movies, beginning with *The Muppet Movie* in 1979.

A L M O N D   G R O V E

Lots in John Mason's 1873 almond orchard northwest of the train station first went on sale Saturday, September 3, 1887, just weeks after the town had officially incorporated. Mason had sold his land to John Bean, Alphonse Wilder, Augustine Nicholson, Fen Massol and Captain Magnus Tait and these five had laid out a grid of streets and water pipes and small, house-sized "town" lots. Banker Wilder had served on the committee which determined the new town's boundaries and Fen Massol would shortly be elected to the equivalent of the town council. They sold 120 lots on that first Saturday and the Almond Grove has been a popular place to live ever since.

LEAFY, TRANQUIL AND FLAT, the Almond Grove invites a stroll or a jog and rewards the eye with a cornucopia of picket fence designs, Queen Anne details and Carpenter Gothic craftsmanship.

84 St. Mary's Catholic Church
219 Bean Avenue
1881, Expansion: **1914**

St. Mary's Catholic Church, originally a mission on North Santa Cruz Avenue at Bean, was moved to its present location in 1913 and expanded the following year. The first outpost was built in 1881, six years before the church established the college now known as the Novitiate. The elementary school was founded under Father Dougherty's tenure in 1954.

St. Mary's

85 Gober House
212 Bean Avenue
c**1876**

Physician Robert P. Gober, John Bean's son in law, served the town until his death in 1943. The Gober and Bean families shared a grand home at the corner of Bean and North Santa Cruz, built by C. F. Scammon and destroyed in 1938. This modest house was hidden behind the larger one. Old timers remember this as the home of "grandfather" Gober, actually the doctor's father.

Grandfather Gober House

86 Dickinson House
107 Wilder Avenue
Cordelia Dickinson (developer), **1910**

There are a large number of Dutch Colonial gambrel roofs in a town supposedly known for Queen Anne cottages and Craftsman bungalows. This house, and its twin at 113, both built by Cordelia Dickinson, are fine examples. Notice the Victorian decoration combined with a Craftsman porch.

Englishman Thomas Ham (1869-1943) and his wife Annie bought the house in 1919. Ham operated a shoe store on North Santa Cruz Avenue until his death.

$300, GOLD COIN, bought the land at 29 Tait from John Weldon Lyndon on July 13, 1882. This stretch of Tait was Montgomery Street at the time, not considered part of the Almond Grove. The simple house was built for David and Caroline Belshee in 1885 and since then it has had at least twenty-two different owners.

87 Bean House
102 Massol Avenue, c**1891**

John Bean (1821-1909) arrived in Santa Clara County from Springfield, Ohio in 1883 and bought an orchard outside town, where he learned first-hand how ineffective the then-current pump technology was for spraying to combat tree scale. He eventually patented his solution, a continuous flow turbine that he called the Bean Spray Magic Pump. Surrounded by Bean's nine-acre orchard, the road to the house was naturally called Bean Avenue. In addition to his role in subdividing the Almond Grove, he also began work in 1891 to provide water service to the town, building a pumping facility across the street from his house.

In 1892, Bean and his wife Emeline sold the house to Sophie Rivers, a ladies' tailor, and by then was living in a veritable mansion on Santa Cruz Avenue (destroyed 1938). Pharmacist and mayor T. E. Johns lived here in the first years of the century.

88 Mountain Spring Pumping Station

HD-76-5

342-356 Bean Avenue
1891-2, 1986, 1996

John Bean formed the Mountain Spring Water Company with his sons-in-law David Crummey and Dr. Robert Gober in 1891. Water was collected in a three million gallon reservoir at the top of Overlook and apparently filtered by the earth until pumped from the ground by this station at the end of Bean Avenue. The facility consists of four brick wells with three-foot-diameter openings at the top, two of which carry mason Harry Perrin's name (see 120).

San Jose Water bought Mountain Spring in 1899 and the reservoir is still in use. The pump station, long discarded, was converted to a residence in 1986 and beautifully restored in 1996.

89 Zientek House

106 Tait Avenue
c**1890**

Beth and Steve Zientek bought this house in 1978 looking for a traditional home—a "house with a parlor with doors," as Beth told the local newspaper.

They worked on the house for the next twelve years. A duplex when they bought it, the couple made it a single family home once more. They added a wraparound front porch, finished the attic and restored the ten-foot (3m) ceilings. Two stories stand out from their experiences. When they removed the horse-hair plaster, the house actually smelled like a stable for a while. And mouldings and decorations that had been removed in the 1950s were unearthed—literally—from a pit in the backyard.

The Zienteks received a Bellringer award in 1987 for their years of loving restoration but they weren't completely finished until they had patched up after the 1989 quake.

107

128 Tait

90 Pearce House
128 Tait Avenue
c**1884**

William L. Pearce, born in England in 1819, came to America in 1848. He bought a ranch in this valley in 1869 and moved to town in 1875. Five children and his wife Louisa helped with the general store he established on Santa Cruz Avenue in 1884, which was successful enough so they could afford to move the family home from its original location behind the store to this quiet street sometime before 1892.

Bartholomew Pearce, named for a sixth child who died young, was the Town Treasurer 1896-98. Louisa Pearce Wilder helped chronicle the family's history, and James Hicks Pearce created a branch of the family grocery business at 308 East Main Street and served on the town council 1902-1906.

136 Tait

91 Templeton Boarding House
136 Tait Avenue
1888 Remodel: Chris Spaulding, **1994**

Thomas Templeton came to Los Gatos for his health—he was diagnosed with tuberculosis in Canada. He arrived with his wife Mary Elizabeth and three young children and managed to build this house in 1888 before succumbing to his disease in 1889. Mary Templeton added a second floor and porch in 1892 and managed their home as a boarding house until 1920.

In 1930, the house became a duplex, and in 1945, a triplex. Today it is once again a single family residence, with an exterior remodel by architect Chris Spaulding in 1994.

108

92 Place House
139 Tait Avenue
1886 Renovation: Gary Schloh, **1988**

The second house built on Tait, this vernacular Victorian shares some features, particularly its half-gable, with Magnus Tait's house one block north. Elvert, the 24-year-old son of furniture and coffin merchant Alexander Place, bought the house in 1887 and George B. was born to Elvert and his wife Emma the following year. The Place family worshipped at St. Luke's, lived in this house for many decades, and George attended Louise Van Meter's first grade class in 1896.

The Place Mortuary moved into the gracious Coggeshall mansion on Santa Cruz Avenue in 1917 (see 14) and George took over from his father to continue the multi-generational tradition in town. Future mayor Pat O'Laughlin and his wife Maggie Kilkenny restored the home in the 1970s (see also 110).

93 Mason House
203 Tait Avenue
c1875

HD-80-1 (Almond Grove)

John S. Mason's home at the center of the Almond Grove predates the streets and the subdivision. Almond Grove represents the last forty of the 162½ acres that Mason purchased from Edward Auzerais in 1865.

A spooky discovery was reportedly made in the backyard: a headstone for a five year old girl named Martha V. Ehrlach with a German inscription and dated January 25, 1882.

94 Smallest House
304 Nicholson Avenue
Gary Schloh, **1996**

When fire damaged the 1920-vintage "granny shack" next to the Mason House, the replacement became, at 514 square feet, one of the smallest houses in the county. To compensate, the house features 13-foot (4m) ceilings and large custom-framed windows.

AN AMERICAN EAGLE clutches this 1987 Bellringer award-winning home's lantern in its beak at 153 Wilder.

Mason House

Smallest House

AUDACIOUS ASYMMETRY, one of the hallmarks of the Queen Anne style, is on display at 135 Tait, a 1983 Gary Schloh project. The original one-story cottage became the second floor above an all-new ground floor. The developer took pains with three-layer moldings and a wrought-iron fence from Kentucky, but the result does not reflect the details of how the Victorian style was interpreted in Los Gatos. Note the simple half-gable. The modest one-story house fit in better with similar roof lines at #139 and #231before it was expanded.

> "At the present time there is scarcely a ten-acre tract along the foothills from Los Gatos north that is not occupied by fruit."
>
> —Pen Pictures from the Garden of the World, 1888.

95 Tait House
231 Tait Avenue
1886

Magnus Tait was born in the Shetland Islands north of Scotland May 30, 1837 and came to America when he was one year old. He fought in the Civil War and was imprisoned in five different Confederate prisoner of war camps, including the dreaded Andersonville. He lived to tell the tale in his book *My Rebel Prison Life*. Captain Tait arrived in Los Gatos in July 1887 and bought the northern edge of John Mason's Almond Grove.

Tait was a miner and a carpenter and an active Baptist (the Baptist church was on West Main Street at the time). When Almond Grove was subdivided, Tait owned the south side of Bachman Avenue from Massol to Santa Cruz, four to seven lots deep. By 1904, he had sold every one, including this house. Tait was a board member of the Los Gatos Building & Loan Association from 1889 to 1920.

The sidewalk with the hitching post outside is one of the area's first—streets in Almond Grove were not paved until 1928. Neighbor Mrs. Howard Burrows, who arrived in 1906, recalls that the sidewalk was a mecca for roller-skaters.

Restoration work in the 1970s turned up an abandoned door on the Tait side, an issue of the San Francisco *Chronicle* dated 1895 tucked in a wall cavity, and involved removing "phony" paneling and yellow paint from clear heart redwood.

EARLY ONE SUNDAY morning, a visitor inquired after an address on Tait. "This is 231," the woman sipping tea on the porch said quietly. "Did you know," the eager visitor asked then, "that this was Magnus Tait's house?" "Yes," she said simply and returned to her tea and her morning.

110

96 M. V. B. Daves House
228 Massol
C. F. Scammon, **1889**

Martin Van Buren Daves, a florist and member of the prominent family for which Daves Avenue is named, commissioned this house from builder C. F. Scammon. In 1894, he sold to Dr. Eleonora "Alice" Yelland, possibly the first female physician in town. Fanciful Berkeley architect W. R. Yelland (1890-1966) was born in Los Gatos—could Dr. Yelland be the architect's mother?

228 Massol

97 Watkins House
328 Bachman Avenue
1885

Fenilen "Fen" Massol apparently owned and possibly built this vernacular Victorian house shortly before joining with four other property owners to subdivide the Almond Grove. Fen's father, Florian A. Massol (1810-1890) had been in the wholesale hardware business with Collis P. Huntington in Sacramento in 1853. He retired in 1869 and came to Los Gatos in 1883. Fen was Florian and Orpha's only son.

328 Bachman

Perhaps equally well-known was the home's second owner, pharmacist Frank F. Watkins. In 1893, Watkins combined his pharmacy with that of Almeron Skinkle to form the Watkins-Skinkle Corner Drug Store at North Santa Cruz and Main Street, under the town's signature cupola. The two partners were also agents for the Sunset Telephone Company. Watkins was a founding director of the Los Gatos Telephone Company in 1910 and he managed its growth 1917-1931.

The unpretentious home may have come from a midwestern farm house pattern book—the steep roof seems designed to handle snow.

BORN IN THE HOUSE GRAND-FATHER BUILT at 124 Wilder, Elayne Shuman of 145 Wilder is something of a neighborhood matriarch—she has lived on this street all her life. The 1989 earthquake destroyed her home, but developer Dave Flick rebuilt it.

ONE OF THREE officially registered home names in town, this one, at 119 Tait, is joined by *Frog Hollow* (89 Fairview, see 83) and *Paradise Found* (399 Nicholson). The owner, speaking with a thick Scottish brogue, wants to live "no place else" than Los Gatos.

GLEN RIDGE

As the town matured, new neighborhoods became fashionable. The brow of land bounding the Almond Grove on the west was developed as Glen Ridge around the turn of the century. The Taylor family of Alameda bought several lots north of Pennsylvania from Frank McCullagh and the street through to Hernandez was known as Taylor Street before 1909. But then A. C. and his wife E. E. Short developed the curving avenue from Hernandez to Nicholson.

The 100 block of Glenridge forms a graceful arc, like the crescents of London, and Short cleverly extended each lot's property five feet (1.5 m) across the street to insure that no future development would block the sunrise view of town and Blossom Hill beyond.

THE LANDLORD LIVES NEXT DOOR. 14 Glenridge was built as a rental house in 1888 by the Hunters, travel agents and owners of #10. Harry S. Topping, vulcanizer, lived here in 1912 with Mrs. Helen Topping at #10. Daisy Melvin was here in 1925 and Edwin Melvin (of the Melvin Funeral Home) built #17 shortly thereafter. William Cotton, the geotechnical engineer, recevied a Bellringer award for restoration work in 1976.

 **98 Urquhart House**
19 Glenridge Avenue
C. F. Scammon (Builder), **1893**

Although it was commissioned by dry goods merchant Charles A. Bronaugh, Dr. Richard A. Urquhart (c1840-1920) and his wife bought the Queen Anne/Eastlake style Victorian shortly after its construction. The Urquharts lived in the house for the next thirty years. Mrs. Urquhart was founder and first president of the History Club in 1897.

The house has had many owners. In the 1960s it was home to Mr. & Mrs. John Hogan, promoters of do-it-yourself stained glass. Prominent San Jose attorney Philip DiNapoli and his wife Jennifer lived here for twenty-five years following the Hogans.

99 Pierce House

20 Glenridge Avenue
1892 Renovation: Gary Schloh, **1997**

Dexter and Cynthia Pierce bought this land from Mr. & Mrs. F. L. Taylor in 1892. They built a boarding house and lived with the tenants. There was a boarder's dining room downstairs. The house became a private residence when the Pierces sold it to Mr. & Mrs. John Schofield in 1914 as Glenridge became too fashionable for multi-family uses.

100 The Bungalow

25 Glenridge Avenue
1898

ONE WORD OR TWO? Is it Glenridge, or Glen Ridge? The street itself says two, but modern usage is one word..

It is still possible that George Hooke's avant garde home, which he called The Bungalow, was designed by famed Berkeley architect Bernard Maybeck. The early Craftsman aesthetic is approximately right and although it seems as if Maybeck did not work in the South Bay before 1900, it is hard to be definitive because Maybeck's office records burned in the San Francisco Fire of 1906.

George H. Hooke was the manager of the successful Los Gatos Canning Company at 57 North Santa Cruz when it began operation in 1882, and he bought the facility outright in 1894. In one season, the cannery produced over a million cans. Hooke sold the plant to the Hunt Brothers in 1906.

LIKE TWO OLD FRIENDS, the Libante House at #33 (right), built by D. C. Crummey, and George Hooke's home, *The Bungalow*, at #25, enjoy the morning sun together as they have for a hundred years. Crummey's house was only alone for five years before Hooke's house joined it.

The Bungalow was one of the first houses in town wired for electricity and the evidence is still visible to all: the porch is decorated with bare light bulbs mounted on the lintels. Sometime after 1912, Hooke sold the house to Andrew and Idah Falch. In 1916, Falch became the editor and publisher of the Los Gatos *Mail-News*. Mr. Falch was always away, it seemed, and neighbors recall the Falch girls noisily roller-skating around and around the wooden porch.

Libante House

Crummey	17 years
Turner	42 years
Libante	47 years

WITH THE RETURN OF THE STAIRS, the 1895 home at 22 Glenridge became its old self, undoing modifications that created a duplex in 1938.

101 Libante House

33 Glenridge Avenue
1893

David C. Crummey was President of the Mountain Spring Water Company, in partnership with his father-in-law, John Bean, when he built his home on a direct line between the water company's reservoir in the hills (which still exists) and the pump facility at the end of Bean Avenue. David's son John would go on to build grandfather Bean's Spray Pump enterprise into the giant conglomerate FMC.

The huge turned wood knobs and cubes of the outside railings are repeated inside. This is one of the first houses with sheet glass windows, one facing east and the other north.

George W. Turner, one of the original directors of the Los Gatos Telephone Company, bought the house in 1909 and his family has never left it. Turner was the equivalent of mayor 1910-1912 when the town dealt with local prohibition and funding the first Town Hall. He and councilmember Doolan often opposed the majority and frequently kept the government from functioning. Perhaps because he was a likeable fellow, Turner did not receive the censure that Doolan did. (George L. Turner, a founder of the Bank of Los Gatos, was apparently no relation.)

The Turner family lived in this house until 1952 when Jean Libante, George's granddaughter, and her husband Andre bought it. Andre's family was well-known for their French Laundry (see 25). Jean and Andre met while students at Los Gatos High School and have lived in town since their marriage in 1947.

"I enjoy telling people that I live in the big Crummey house on Glenridge..."
— Andre Libante

POWER POSITION at the corner of Glenridge and Hernandez is occupied by this imposing shingled Craftsman bungalow built in 1909-10 by E. E. Pomeroy. Mayor and banker James J. Stanfield (see 27) was the home's second owner and banker S. D. Balch its third.

102 Decker House
75 Glenridge Avenue
c1910 Renovation: John Miller, 1998

Town of Los Gatos Planning Commissioner Sandy Decker and her husband Gil went to extraordinary lengths to restore this neglected and heavily earthquake-damaged Craftsman to its original glory. The columns in front were redwood logs (with bark) from trees on the property dating to the late 1940s, but they could not be saved. Instead, the trunks were milled on site and used to trim the interior.

BICOASTAL CRAFTSMAN built by Lillie and Bert Welch at 115 Glenridge in 1911 seems to reflect an Atlantic aesthetic.

103 Osborne House
121 Glenridge Avenue
c1912

A Dutch Colonial style home, with its trademark gambrel roof turned to face the morning sun, built in the 1910s by Pennsylvania Dutchman Dr. Antrim Edgar Osborne (1856-1935) and his wife Margaret (Paxton). Dr. Osborne, a physician and a psychiatrist, was instrumental in creating the California Home for Feeble-minded Children in Santa Clara and was elected to the State Senate in 1920.

Upon his return to private life, Dr. Osborne was a strong advocate—in 1927—for the city manager form of government which Los Gatos has employed since the early 1950s. He was President of the Historical Society and made one of the first studies of the local Ohlone Indians.

121 Glenridge

104 Crider Mansion
145 Glenridge Avenue
1908

This stately colonial manor was built in 1908 by businessman E. R. Strome of North Dakota for his retirement. Meanwhile, in 1914, merchant J. Walter Crider built a more modern home at 25 Hernandez (see 113). By 1920, with Crider's Department Store now filling the Ford Opera House, councilman (and soon, Mayor) Crider and his wife Lydia moved their family to this more dignified home. Mrs. Crider was still at this address in 1967.

In the 1970s, the original marble lions flanking the steps were spirited off to Colorado by former owner Luke Little, who claimed he had no indication that they were historical.

BUILT FOR A BRIDE who refused to live in it (the story goes), hardware store owner Osmer Lewis' 1902 house at 139 Glenridge (right) has been called bad luck. It is hard to imagine anyone who wouldn't feel lucky to live on this sunny street.

INDIVIDUALISTIC ROOFS, like wildflowers, seem to seek the sun at 133 Glenridge. A Craftsman cottage, it was built by David Crummey in 1909 but owned by J. Rea Bryant, "dealer in all kinds of lumber and millwork," after 1910.

105 Green House
211 Glenridge Avenue
1909

George Anthony Green (1873-1957) and his wife Edith Stahl (1882-1927) came to Los Gatos in 1904 and built this Craftsman cottage in 1909. The couple had three children.

Green, who held a degree in pharmaceuticals from the University of California at Berkeley, operated Green's Drug Store for decades after buying T. E. Johns' interest in the Johns and Johnson Drug Store. Elected to the Board of Trustees, as the council was called in 1922, he became the first official mayor of the town in 1927 when the state mandated a change in nomenclature. Annoyed by the criticism of the town's decision to pave

Almond Grove in concrete rather than asphalt, he called for a recall election as a plebiscite on the issue. The voters resoundingly rejected his offer to resign and the popular druggist served a total of twenty years on the council.

The gable faces the street, but the plan is turned, leaving the front door to face the side yard. The current owners have kept the kitchen remarkably authentic by cleverly hiding the modern appliances inside vintage cabinetry that opens in surprising ways.

CLEVER KITCHEN (left and above); dining room (below); living room (lower right); entry (lower left).

AMERICAN GOTHIC house at the bend of Overlook Road could have served as the model for Grant Wood's famous painting. The 1890s house of Andrew and Adelia Gerlach earned a Bellringer award in 1976.

The heights to the west of Almond Grove and Glenridge merge with the hillside homes of Monte Sereno; the boundaries are arbitrary, defined by a meandering creek which could have been spanned if desired. The 120-acre ranch of Frank McCullagh, the developer of Fairview, was sold on August 26, 1887 to Dr. Handy, G. W. Lynch, Alfred Malpas and others, netting $60,000 for his 120 acres. These properties became the lattice of streets such as Pennsylvania, Palm, Walnut, and Chestnut. McCullagh and his wife were homesick for Philadelphia and their home on Wissahickon Avenue, so they made sure that their home in Los Gatos was at the same intersection as it had been on the east coast—Live Oak and Wissahickon.

Today the road to Saratoga runs straight through, but in Los Gatos' first decades, the road made an abrupt jog south at Quito Road to avoid the Los Gatos Wine & Fruit plant (1885-1919) at what was then known as Austin Corners. Alfred Malpas, the manager of the plant, built a fine home in the hills south of the plant which we now think of as overlooking Los Gatos to the east rather than Austin Corners to the north. The electric interurban lines came from Saratoga down this road (1903-1933), and stopped at a Japanese resort named Nippon Mura (now La Hacienda hotel).

106 La Estancia   HD-73-4
18000 Overlook Road
c1880 Renovation: Willis Polk, J. R. Tobin (builder), 1901

In 1894, Mr. and Mrs. Frank McCullagh, the original owners of 138 acres between Lyndon's acreage around Broadway to the south and B. F. Bachman's 50 acres to the north, returned from Philadelphia. After creating Fairview Plaza and streets like Pennsylvania, Wissahickon and Laurel with their 1880s-era subdivision, the homesick couple had moved back to the East Coast in 1887.

They re-purchased their 1880 house and six and a half acres and commissioned young San Francisco architect Willis Jefferson Polk to expand and remodel it. Polk (1867-1924) had earned a

reputation as a brilliant but erratic designer quick to criticize traditional work by others. Through his articles in the *California Architect*, Polk is credited with encouraging the use of mission themes. For the McCullagh's, he proposed a replica of Mission San Miguel Archangel.

Polk, with George Washington Percy assisting, cut the original house in two and had it pulled apart by teams of horses. An arcaded loggia was inserted between the halves and "Polk's design obliterated all visual evidence of the original fabric," in the words of architectural historian Richard Longstreth.

Mary Evans McCullagh was an avid horticulturist, and water from the Mountain Spring reservoir above their home made it possible for her to create lavish gardens, including redwoods, a Cedar of Lebanon and a towering cypress. *La Estancia* (the ranch), as she called it, was selected in 1902 by House & Garden magazine as the first west coast home ever reviewed. Dr. and Mrs. W. Horace Jones made this house their home from 1939, when the McCullaghs passed away, until the 1960s. When the present owners found it in 1980, it was one of only three Polk-designed homes in the county and was scheduled for destruction. Most of the plants were dead. Today the house and two acre garden are a showpiece, featured on a recent Garden Tour.

211 Alexander Avenue

MODEST MEDITERRANEAN
Revival home at 207 Belmont, renovated by John Miller, was the home of the Deckers before they remodeled the Craftsman at 75 Glenridge (see 102).

381 Pennsylvania

363 Pennsylvania

FEROCIOUS INTERIORS by local designer Valerie Irene Zacher. The owner provided the mounted heads and two full zebra pelts (with hooves on). Place settings are etched into the glass counter off the kitchen. The grand house offered. "a magnificent backdrop for adding touches of the original and the bizarre," Ms. Zacher offers.

107 Van Denburg Estate

Address Withheld
c1875 Renovation: c1972
Remodeling: Krista Wendt, Valerie Irene Zacher, 1997

The hunting lodge of Daniel Van Denberg (1824-1911), a San Francisco dentist, situated on over twenty acres west of town, was likely begun as a small cabin in the 1860s or 1870s. Dr. Van Denberg was a dentist practicing in San Francisco who arranged to spend more and more of his time at his Los Gatos property in the 1880s with his wife Elizabeth and their three children. The estate expanded to include a large koi pond, several fountains, trails, and a large barn. The three-story main house features redwood wainscoting throughout, clipped ceilings on the top floor, etched glass and a ballroom.

In July, 1885, the dentist hired a 23-year-old Japanese immigrant named Masatsune Ichinoi as a gardener. Ichinoi studied English for two hours every afternoon for a year; once the language barrier was breached, the daily lessons began to focus on dentistry. In 1889, Ichinoi left to study dental surgery in Philadelphia. Dr. Ichinoi (1862-1929) returned to Japan in 1894 and was honored in 1992 by the Japan Society of Dental Medicine History for his contributions of laughing gas and prosthodontics.

The property was sold for the first time in the 1940s and has had few owners. Neglected, the once-grand lodge was slated for demolition in the early 1970s when it was rescued from oblivion by the current owners.

108 Steinbeck House

16250 Greenwood Lane, Monte Sereno
Laurence Case (builder), **1934**

A GRACEFUL STATUE guards the Van Denburg estate's koi pond, adjacent to the spacious and shady picnic area.

John Ernst Steinbeck (1902-1968) called his 800-square foot house, in what was then the western suburbs of Los Gatos, *Arroyo del Ajo*, or Garlic Gulch, in reference to the cooking of his Italian neighbors. Steinbeck's first wife, Carol Henning, helped design the cottage which was built by local contractor Laurence Case. They moved in at the height of the Great Depression, in the year in which utopian reformer Upton Sinclair lost his second bid for governor to conservative forces. Sinclair's EPIC (End Poverty In California) platform surely echoed Steinbeck's sentiments.

His fourth novel, *Tortilla Flat*, with its stinging characterizations of some of the people of Monterey peninsula, may have been among Steinbeck's reasons for moving here from Pacific Grove in 1934. His mother died that year, and his father passed away a year later.

Steinbeck wrote the novella *Of Mice and Men* on the front patio and in the living room of the guest house, but his puppy ate the manuscript and he was forced to recreate it from memory. "I was pretty mad," he later wrote, "but the poor fellow may have been acting critically." Local historian Kathryn Morgan says that he wrote perhaps his best-known work, *The Grapes of Wrath* during a few short disciplined hot summer months. It was released in 1939, the year that a former EPIC candidate was elected governor.

Fame and prosperity forced the future Nobel laureate to build a fence. Morgan writes that one stage mother had her child dance on the writer's lawn in hopes of an introduction to Hollywood. Houses were being built in the area. Steinbeck told a friend, "the noise is driving us nuts," and the couple moved to a 47-acre parcel in the Santa Cruz Mountains. Even after the move, Steinbeck was sometimes seen at the Lyndon Hotel bar, where on one occasion he reportedly entertained director John Ford and Charlie Chaplin.

THE FIRST FLOOR WAS A BARN, actually the Van Denburg estate's carriage house. The views from the third floor are stunning.

The original redwood board-and-batten house has been expanded and painted white. Although the home's current owner tried to put the home on the National Register of Historic Places in 1989, he won a seat on the Monte Sereno city council in 1996 on a platform of easing historic preservation restrictions. The house is nearly impossible to find and the owner, like Steinbeck himself, wants to keep it that way. Steinbeck tourists should visit the National Steinbeck Center, One Main Street, Salinas, California, which holds a Steinbeck Festival each August.

121

The Gables

METAL DEER GRAZE where the flower-eating variety are deliberately fenced out.

Henry Ford and Thomas Edison stayed overnight at homes in this neighborhood in October 1915.

109 The Gables
60 Ellenwood Avenue
1919

Jemima Ann Templeman Bogart (c1855-1926) built this beautiful mansion a few years after the death of her husband, hardware merchant Arthur Wellington Bogart (c1843-1916). Mr. Bogart owned two hardware stores in San Francisco, one in San Jose, and another on North Santa Cruz Avenue.

Arthur arrived in San Francisco from Nova Scotia in 1869 and there married Jemima Templeman of Lynn, Massachusetts. They summered in Los Gatos at a house on Los Gatos Boulevard that they called *Sleepy Oaks*.

Recent owners named the estate *The Gables*, perhaps referring to the entertainment pavilion which Julia Morgan designed for the Hearst compound, Wyntoon. Notice the tiny informal park across from the house with its juxtaposed benches and a drinking fountain.

110 Villa Tusculum
🔔 HR-7
54 Chestnut
1894

Mr. and Mrs. G. M. Meriam named their imposing Eastlake-style mansion *Villa Tusculum* after a neighborhood which overlooks Rome. Mr. Meriam (1843-1897), a retired lumberman, and his wife, Emma (1846-1896), built the house of redwood and included modern features such as pocket doors. The family built the carriage house (now the residence at 52 Chestnut) first and lived there almost two years during construction of the main house. Local legend has it that the Meriam's daughter ended up marrying the contractor.

Sadly, if the available record is correct, Emma died when the house was two years old and Mr. Meriam passed away just one year later. The turret roof was probably originally taller and more bulbous, in keeping with the Eastlake style (compare the turret at 114). Future mayor Patrick O'Laughlin and his wife Maggie Kilkenny were awarded a Bellringer plaque for their restoration work in 1987 (see also 92).

111 Petrek House
15 Chestnut Avenue
c**1910**

Sharing their home comes naturally to Catherine and John Petrek. They remodeled their home at 325 Johnson before this, and the process, for them, involves exchanging knowledge with other restoration veterans.

Petrek House

Finding only a narrow, winding staircase to the second floor tucked partially under the eaves, they dismembered the balustrade to get furniture to the bedrooms. Methodically, the details were resolved. A ceilingpaper to simulate pressed tin on the lofty ceilings, glass front cabinets to lighten the kitchen, period wallpapers and moldings cut with a custom knife for the replacement stair railing.

The style of this house is transitional—the towers and gables are reminiscent of Queen Anne, but the simple details, particularly

123

the living room windows, are early Craftsman style. In keeping with the turn-of-the-century brio, the Petreks chose a striking deep blue for the exterior.

RESTORING A VICTORIAN home can take years. A roll of stiff embossed wallpaper border called "Lincrusta," typical of the unusual authentic and replacement materials required for accuracy, is ready to finish off the dining room of the Petrek House at 15 Chestnut. The Petreks have since completed the project.

THE TOWN BOUNDARY was the backyard property line of the 1896 summer cottage at 5 Palm, a 1976 Bellringer.

MINISTER PLENIPOTENTIARY of the British Diplomatic Corps, Edward Loftus was assigned to the Kingdom of Siam before retiring to the 1910-era Craftsman at 16 Chestnut Avenue in 1935. Notice the fabulous oak in the driveway and the cut stone curb along Chestnut.

112 Pierce House

9 Peralta Avenue
1888-92 Renovation: Gary Schloh, **1989**

James C. Crosby, a brick and stone mason, bought this land, with its broad frontage on Pennsylvania Avenue, in 1888. He built a house, reportedly using stone from the same Almaden quarry that supplied Stanford University's builders. Records show that he sold the house and a water tower to Mary Pierce in 1891. In 1907, a Mrs. M. D. Pierce commissioned famed architect Julia Morgan to design a home in Berkeley. In 1914, the same Mrs. Pierce built a second Julia Morgan-designed home at "Penn and Peralta," which scholars thought demolished. Was this house remodeled by the brilliant Morgan, a year before she designed the Saratoga Women's Foothill Club?

Duane and Denise Billheimer received a Bellringer award for the house in 1987 and the family repaired extensive earthquake damage two years later.

Pierce House

GEOMETRIC NATURE was a
theme of the stained glass that
Frank Lloyd Wright designed for
his buildings. Stalks of wheat or
hollyhocks were all made to con-
form to straight lines and diamond
patterns. This beautiful window
pays homage to Wright's motifs.

113 Franklin House
25 Hernandez Avenue
1914

Commissioned by dry goods merchant J. Walter Crider in 1914, this unusual house is likely the town's only prairie-style building. Frank Lloyd Wright invented the style, which features horizontal lines and wide, cantilevered roof overhangs. The clean lines and details, such as the block pilaster caps, make the design decades ahead of its time. The work of Michael Graves in the 1980s and 1990s re-introduced this type of simplified ornamentation, for example. Another authentic feature is that the front door does not align with the steps—visitors must turn twice to reach the entry.

In 1916, Mr. Crider bought Ford's Opera House and expanded his line to create Crider's Department Store. In 1919, the mercantilist was elected to the town council (he would serve as the equivalent of Mayor 1922-24) and the family moved, in 1920, to the grand colonial house on Glenridge known as the Crider Mansion (see 104). The Criders sold to prominent local physician Blake Franklin and his wife Mary. Dr. Franklin had offices in the La Cañada building, was President of the Chamber of Commerce, and wrote a column for the Los Gatos *Mail-News*.

IT'S BIGGER THAN IT LOOKS.
Judge Fowler's 1891 Queen Anne
cottage at 19 Hernandez is now
three stories and 2,500 square
feet. The judge's daughter, Miss
Edna Fowler, a Deputy Recorder,
also lived here. Observers note
the cross-gabled hip roof and the
sunburst motif in the decoration of
this 1976 Bellringer home.

125

114 Malpas House HR-11

55 Hernandez Avenue
Charles Scammon (builder), **1887**
Restoration: Tim Lentz (builder), **1991-93**

Alfred Malpas had been a printer and telegraph operator for the railroad before enlisting in the New Jersey volunteer infantry to fight the Civil War in 1861. Alfred fought in both battles of Bull Run and was wounded in the second. He returned to the railroad after the war, but in 1868 he traveled to the Orient for his health. By the time he returned to San Francisco, the transcontinental railroad had arrived and he worked for the Central Pacific until his retirement in 1884. Malpas, his wife Mary "Bessie" and their two sons and daughters were living on their 187-acre ranch in Saratoga when the family bought a portion of Frank McCullagh's 120-acre ranch and commissioned this avant garde $25,000 residence, then well west of the town limits. Malpas later managed the Los Gatos Wine & Fruit Company's plant at Austin Corners (Saratoga and Quito Roads).

The fourteen-room house had two bathrooms, one upstairs and one down, with piped-in hot and cold water and gas heating throughout. The gas was manufactured in the basement from gasoline. The house has a basement and about five thousand square feet of living space. As reported in a 1976 newspaper article, features included hand-painted ceilings, a white oak staircase and paintings by Mr. and Mrs. Gustave Fassin, internationally-known artists who lived here at one time.

A member of the Macabee (gopher trap) family lived here briefly before the Reverend Lawrence Taylor bought the house in 1947. In one shattering moment just after 5 p. m. October 17, 1989, the second floor tumbled onto the first, briefly trapping Taylor's daughter Lysbet Wright and wreaking hundreds of thousands of dollars worth of damage to the massive old house. Lysbet's mother, Kay Taylor, arranged to have their home restored, but both survivors passed away in the 1990s, leaving a messy and public legal fight over ownership of the building, which had been beautifully restored by Tim Lentz.

115 Short House
130 Hernandez Avenue
A. C. Short, **1895**

Short House

A. C. Short built his home using redwood trees which grew on his property in the Santa Cruz mountains. Built on nearly one acre, the Queen Anne house includes a fireplace in the cozy entry and a large room on the third floor which includes the turret. Some walls are simply 1 x 12 redwood planks covered with building felt and wallpaper.

The home's ghost is named George and causes all new clocks brought into the house to malfunction.

A. C. developed the Glenridge area in the 1900s, particularly the graceful curve of the 100 block. His wife, Ellen E. Short subdivided the Glenwood Terrace neighborhood west of Bachman Park (leaving her name on Ellenwood Avenue). We speculate that A. C.'s name was Alexander (another street in the subdivision). His brother, W. C. Short, served Los Gatos as the equivalent of Mayor 1916-18.

116 Hamsher House
17940 Saratoga Road
1890, Expansion: **1999-2000**

Built by a wagon manufacturer named Mitchell, this home is famous as the home (1922-1950s) of Los Gatos' first historian, Clarence F. Hamsher of the First National Bank, and his son, W. R. "Bob" Hamsher, Town Treasurer (1948-64) and tireless civic volunteer.

The 3,100 square foot, 13-room house is expanding. The current owners bought it in 1972 and installed a pool but kept the water tank. At 37 feet (11.25m), the new tower required a special variance from the town of Monte Sereno.

EDELEN DISTRICT

DAPPLED SUNSHINE lights the pastel-colored example of straight-forward cottage architecture at 118 University Avenue.

CLASSICAL OR VICTORIAN or something inbetween, the "free classical"-style home at 128 University combines a Greek pediment and classical symmetry with the insouciance of a Queen Anne.

John Miles, a winter visitor from Quebec, bought the vineyard north of the grammar school with his friend, a Mr. Edelen, in 1886, shortly after his first visit to Los Gatos. The northern boundary of the Miles-Edelen subdivision, which they called The Vineyards, was a diagonal railroad track—a spur track that served Forbes Mill.

The Edelen District offers the charm of Almond Grove but in a smaller package more closely related to the downtown. If Almond Grove is Walk to Town, Edelen is almost Be in Town. The neighborhood incorporates all the homes between the business district and the freeway. Before the freeway, there were reportedly many homes east of Edelen Avenue on the banks of the creek, but they were subject to nearly annual flooding. Today, the town uses the space between Highway 17 and the creek as its "backstage"—the R. J. Bryant Corporation Yard.

117 Skinkle House
129 Edelen Avenue
Francis W. Reid, **1892**

Francis Reid, a 29-year-old architect, built this late Queen Anne and sold it two years later to George L. Turner, the President of the Bank of Los Gatos, who in turn sold it to pharmacist Almeron Skinkle, Jr. and his wife Katie in 1897. The Skinkles came to Los Gatos from the midwest (they were married in Nebraska) in 1891. Almeron established a drug store on West Main Street at about the same time that Frank Watkins opened one on Santa Cruz Avenue. By 1894, the Watkins-Skinkle corner drug store had been established under the turret of the Hofstra Block (now called the La Cañada Building—see 7).

In 1898, the Skinkle's daughter Mimi was the first editor of *Lambda Gamma* (Greek letters "L" and "G"), the Los Gatos High School newspaper. The High School was then located alongside the grammar school, just a block away. Katie Skinkle died in 1904, at age 47, and the family moved away. Max Walden owned the house in sixties while he converted the old grammar school to the Old Town retail center.

The current owners, Mr. and Mrs. Murphy, bought the house in 1995. Pamela Murphy is co-owner of Elle d'Lin Design and the home's interiors reflect her firm's abilities.

129

John Miles house

118 Miles House
130 Edelen Avenue
1886

John Charles Miles (1850-1918), one of the developers of the Edelen district, built this beautiful Queen Anne shingle-style home in 1886. A winter resident for 33 years, he spent summers at Old Orchard, Maine. The current owners bought and restored the home in 1963, and in 1970 it was used as a location for a motion picture starring Orson Welles. A minor horror movie also starring Pamela Franklin, the film has been released as both *The Toy Factory* and *Necromancy*. In 1997, the house was the scene of a television movie production.

Harry Perrin house

120 Perrin House   HD-73-7
315 University Avenue
Harry Perrin (builder), **1896**

An example of a tradition called a "honeymoon house," in which the wedding follows the construction of a suitable residence for the new couple. Brickmason Harry Perrin built this solid home for his bride, Theresa Clinkinbeard, in 1896. Harry, of English-Irish descent, was born in Bangor, Maine in 1858. Theresa was one of eleven children. The house had no electricity initially, but the brick walls were fitted with piping for gas lighting. Mr. Perrin had a hand in the Mountain Springs Water Company Pump House at the end of Bean Avenue (1892, see 88) and later built the revetments (fortifications) for the San Francisco Presidio.

A rare example of rusticated Romanesque style applied to a residence, the home was renovated in 1958 and converted to offices in 1972. The first restorers called their home The Castle. The building inspired a software company tenant to name itself Red Brick Systems. The woodwork in the house is black walnut, now painted white. It was a boarding house in the 1930s, and every room has a door to the hall.

BLACK WALNUT WOODWORK has been painted white, but it is still the original wood. The interiors are brighter than in Victorian times, as well.

130   *Perrin entry*

121 Lawson Scott House
321 University Avenue
1893 Remodeled: c**1991**

An example of Folk Victorian style, the Lawson Scott house is known to old-timers as the home of Jack Vodden, who lived here from the 1920s until 1987. Vodden worked for Sterling Lumber (now the New Old Town, 23) for twenty years and then co-founded El Gato Building Materials (currently Campo di Bocce, 153)

The three-story home has been completely remodeled and given a new foundation. Brick from the foundation was recycled for backyard landscaping.

321 University

122 Maria's Berry Farm
41 Miles Avenue
John Lien, **1992**

In 1992, Maria's Berry Farm lay squarely in the path of progress. In this case, it was threatened by the construction of Highway 85. Originally near Winchester Avenue and Knowles Drive, the town declared the structures historic, thus forcing the California Transportation Department to pay for their relocation. A trellis connects the two-story house with the water tower.

THE TOWN'S CORPORATION yard is named for Robert J. Bryant, an arborist and Director of Parks, Forestry and Maintenance Services for many years until his retirement in 1993. The odd shapes are surplus light poles. The baseball diamond and the Los Gatos Creek Trail are visible in the background.

LOS GATOS HAS GROWN from one square mile to over ten, from a steady population of about 3,500 to almost 34,000, including unincorporated areas. In other words, the population density of the little boom town has been extended to a region ten times the original size.

6 Environs

The Environs of Los Gatos lead to surrounding communities such as Monte Sereno and Saratoga to the west, Campbell to the north and the southern portions of San Jose to the east. Interesting places, to be sure, but our focus is Los Gatos itself. Los Gatos was established in 1887 as a one square mile town surrounded by farm lands and grew in the 1950s primarily in response to the rapid approach of the boundary with San Jose. San Jose threatened to annex Los Gatos in the 1950s as it had Willow Glen in 1937.

Comfortable county residents to the west of Los Gatos viewed the "fight growth with growth" strategy with alarm and voted, in effect, to secede from Los Gatos in 1957. Taking their name from the mountain to the south, the tranquil new community called itself Monte Sereno. Rather than lose their individualism, Campbell incorporated in 1952 and Saratoga followed suit in 1956.

Los Gatos is the commercial center for thousands of mountain residents, as well, on Black Road, Bear Creek Road, Old Santa Cruz Highway, and in communities such as Aldercroft Heights. There is architecture and history in the mountains, too, but we draw the line at the ridge just south of town.

This final chapter circles the town, dealing first with the mountains to the south, then with lands to the east along Shannon and Kennedy Roads. Los Gatos Boulevard is paid attention, and then we cross Los Gatos Creek at Oak Meadow. We look at Northside—the district north of downtown—and conclude with the former farm lands in the northwest.

CONTENTS

Los Gatos Creek

133

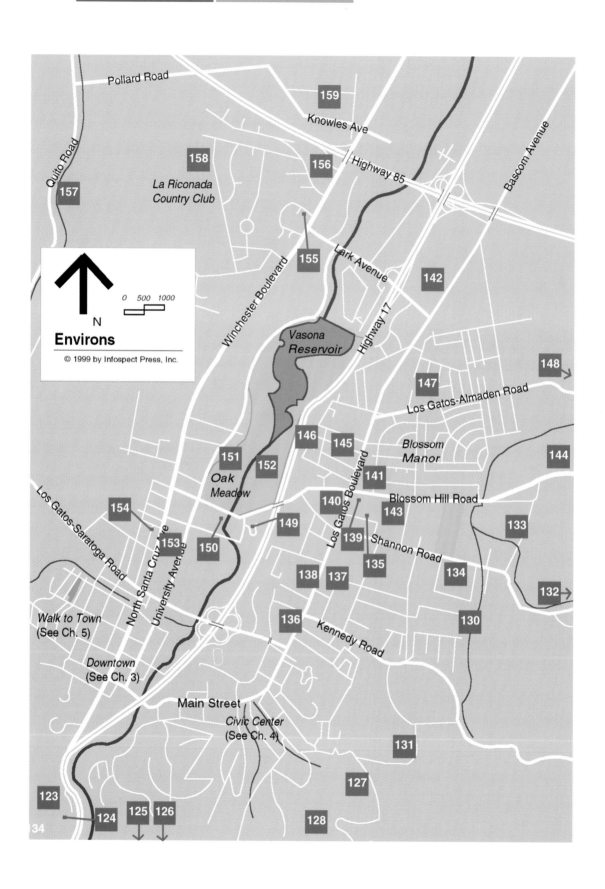

Pollard Road

Quito Road

159

Knowles Ave

158

156

Highway 85

Bascom Avenue

La Riconada
Country Club

157

155

Lark Avenue

142

N

0   500   1000

Environs

© 1999 by Infospect Press, Inc.

Winchester Boulevard

Vasona
Reservoir

Highway 17

148

147

Los Gatos-Almaden Road

146

145

144

151

152

Blossom
Manor

Oak
Meadow

Los Gatos Boulevard

141

Blossom Hill Road

154

140

143

133

153

149

150

139

Shannon Road

Los Gatos-Saratoga Road

North Santa Cruz Ave

University Avenue

138

137

135

134

132

Walk to Town
(See Ch. 5)

136

Kennedy Road

130

Downtown
(See Ch. 3)

Main Street

Civic Center
(See Ch. 4)

131

127

123

128

124   125   126

34

SIERRA AZUL

The mountains that form the town's scenic backdrop are called the Sierra Azul (blue mountains) and rise 900 to 3000 feet (275 to 915m) above the town. For a hundred years, they were protected against the hand of man by their remoteness. In the 1950s, however, developer John Loy created the Montezuma Hills tract and houses reached the highest ridge visible from town along the road named Aztec Ridge by the developer. The exclusive community has attracted several celebrities, including Albert Hakim, implicated in the Reagan-era Iran-Contra scandal, and Olympic figure-skating gold medal winner Peggy Fleming. Steve Wozniak, creator of the Apple computer, has two houses in the hills south and east of Los Gatos.

The Modir Estate

In 1972, Santa Clara County voters created the Mid-Peninsula Regional Open Space District (http://www.openspace.org), which has acquired over 41,000 acres in 23 preserves from Los Gatos to San Carlos. Aztec Ridge meets the Open Space property at the Modir Estate (right), which is particularly audacious and visible from most points in town.

123 Leo & Leona   HD-73-8
17525 Santa Cruz Highway
Robert Treat Paine (sculptor), 1920

SYMBOLS OF THE TOWN, Robert Paine's concrete cats mark the entrance to Poet's Canyon.

Two eight-foot-tall concrete statues, now the official symbols of the Town of Los Gatos, guard the entrance to Poet's Canyon and the road leading to the Wood estate. Colonel Erskine Scott Wood (1852-1944) and his second wife Sara Bard Field (1883-1974), both poets, commissioned the statues in admiration of the species and to demonstrate the value of public art. They have explained patiently that they were not trying to literally symbolize Los Gatos, the cats.

Colonel Wood is described as a "poet and Indian fighter," but was also a wealthy Portland lawyer when he moved to Los Gatos in 1919. His most famous book, *Heavenly Discourse* (1927), tells the stories that celebrities of the time might offer St. Peter as they

THE CATS, the Erskine Scott Wood Estate, is not accessible to the public.

entered heaven. In the twenties, Wood hoped to write a biography of his father, a Civil War physician and friend of Ulysses S. Grant, but his fortune was diminished by the 1929 stock market crash and the book was not completed.

Sculptor Robert Paine came from New York to contribute to the lavish decoration of the 1915 Panama-Pacific Exposition in San Francisco and apparently it was he who approached the Woods. Paine's résumé included apprenticeship under Augustus Saint Gaudens in Chicago and the enlargement of two chariots atop the King Victor Emmanuel monument in Rome (1911-1913). He was given a shack on site and paid a laborer's wage to sculpt the two cats.

Paine studied wildcats at the San Francisco Zoo and invented a sort of three-dimensional pantograph which allowed him to scale his model to full size. Originally painted "a very soft, pale brown," according to Ms. Field, the statues repeatedly fell victim to a series of Halloween pranks. A November 1930 newspaper reports "A reward is offered for the vandals who painted and mutilated Col. Wood's cat statues."

As the Woods would have wanted, the cats are still easily accessible to the public. The two cats are not the same. Dr. Bruce and Diane Ogilvie bought the estate in the 1950s and named the statues Leo and Leona. Visitors are welcome to speculate which is the female—the slit-eyed feline on the right or the more alert cat on the left. (The Ogilvies consider Leo the sleepy cat.) Notice the initials CESW and SBF etched into each cat's base.

124 The Cats Restaurant
17533 Santa Cruz Highway
c1896

THE CATS RESTAURANT, a roadhouse just off Highway 17.

Heavily remodeled during its century of existence, The Cats has been a restaurant and bar just outside town since 1967. Originally a stagecoach stop, it was reportedly a popular place for drivers to bring ladies from town for private assignations. The building has previously been a gun shop, a real estate office and a biker bar. However, it is a myth, say the current owners, that the building has ever housed a bordello.

http://www.lupin.com

125 Lupin Naturist Club
Santa Cruz Mountains
1936

The Santa Cruz Mountains have an unfettered, faintly utopian lure for some, and the Lupin facility, an example of what used to be called a "nudist colony," fits in well. Set on 110 secluded acres in the hills just south of Lexington Reservoir, Lupin's facilities include swimming, hot tub, trails, volleyball, camping and several yurts available for rental.

Introductory tours (reservations required) are offered 10 a. m. to noon, Wednesday, Saturday and Sunday. Wear comfortable footwear and a smile—and bring a towel as "an all-purpose security blanket until the novelty of nudity fades." The Lupin Clubhouse Restaurant serves breakfast, lunch, dinner, and snacks.

The Los Gatos-Saratoga *Times-Observer* noted that the August 1955 convention of the Western Sunbathing Association brought 800 nudists to Los Gatos, and reported that a low-flying plane crashed with no injuries near the volleyball court. Four other voyeurs were given a choice of jail or nudity by some of the more "husky" nudists, and all chose to disrobe and enjoy the weekend.

http://www.parkhere.org/prkpages/lex.htm

126 James J. Lenihan Dam
Lexington Reservoir
1952

Lexington Reservoir was built by the Santa Clara County Water Conservation District as part of a program to capture winter rain for use recharging aquifers and wells in the valley. That is, the water is not used directly, but instead seeps into the ground and is pumped from wells closer to the bay.

The dam was bitterly opposed by some, particularly residents of the communities of Alma and Lexington, which were wiped off the map by the 475-acre Lexington Reservoir. However, the project was funded by over $3 million in publicly-approved bonds. Safety concerns were borne out in 1962, when high water damaged the rim of the 195-foot (60 m) earthen-filled dam. In 1997, the dam was renamed to honor retired Water District director Lenihan, who was not involved in the dam's initial construction.

A SIMPLE SIGN marks the entrance to Los Gatos' low-key nudist colony.

LEXINGTON RESERVOIR holds 19,384 acre-feet of water.

137

127 Yung See San Fong

HD-83-1

16600 Cypress Way
1916-17

Sanborn Young (1873-1964) brought his bride, poet and playwright Ruth Comfort Mitchell (1883-1954), back to the town of her youth in 1916 after her first play was presented on Broadway. The shingled four-story home comprises 5,000 square feet, including a 20' x 44' (6 x 13.5m) living room, and was reportedly built using Chinese labor, on land given as a wedding gift by Ruth's father. *Yung See San Fong* means (by some accounts) "Young's view of the hills." A Chinese proverb associated with the house up the winding Cypress Way states that "The devil can never follow you home if the road takes many turns."

The unusual late-Craftsman house was featured in the December 1918 *Sunset* magazine, which later published many of Mrs. Young's poems. Mrs. Young kept many animals, including her pet deer Lo Lo Mi. In 1921, the Youngs donated a parcel next to Town Hall to the town and, in 1925, Sanborn Young was elected to the State Senate where he served until 1938. Their friend, President Herbert Hoover, visited occasionally.

The current owner, with help from former Los Gatos mayor Mardi Bennett, placed the house on the National Register of Historic Places (83001240) in 1983.

The devil can never follow you home if the road takes many turns...

The 880 square foot living room includes Chinese sayings as decoration.

138

THE NATURAL SIERRA AZUL

Los Gatos is not all man-made—and the natural environment of the Sierra Azul can be fascinating. The mountains form a barrier to the coastal fog known as a thermal belt—a slope from which cold air drains—that is quite visible as the roiling clouds occasionally pour over the ridgeline.

The hills are covered with chaparral—hardy, drought-resistant brush common in California. *Arctostaphylos*, or Manzanita, is known for its smooth red to purple bark. *Arbutus mensiesii*, or Madrone, a shrub-tree that can grow quite tall, is also known for its bark—it is reddish-brown and peels in thin flakes. Thorny blackberry vines are also found in abundance—birds and other animals love the berries and scatter the seeds. *Cytisus scoparius*, or Scotch Broom, is aggressively crowding out native plants all over the state. Its wandlike green stems bloom with small golden yellow flowers in spring and early summer. Another familiar plant is *Heteromeles arbutifolia*, which sports small white flowers in June and bright red berries November to January. It's known as Christmas Berry, California Holly, or Toyon.

Quercus agrifolia

Poison Oak

Unfortunately, Poison Oak (*Rhus*) abounds in the hills around Los Gatos. The three-leaflet leaves, with scallops not points, are rusty red or shiny green and bright red in the fall. Leafless in the winter, the ubiquitous plant continues to secrete irritating oils. Another plant found in abundance is the cheerful *Eschscholzia californica*, the California Poppy. The wildflowers are pale yellow to deep orange and they close at night.

The tree most representative of the area is probably the *Quercus agrifolia*, or Coast Live Oak. The spreading limbs and dense small leaves of this evergreen oak offer a shady rest on a grassy hillside. *Quercus lobata*, or Valley Oak, and *Betulaceae*, or Alder, are usually found near water. Another local tree is the *Umbellularia californica*, known as a Bay or Laurel tree, identified by its long, fragrant, pointed leaves. The Laurel is evergreen but drops yellow and tan leaves in the fall.

Mule deer (family *Cervid*) inhabit these hills and often munch on residential landscaping. In the wild, they eat leaves, grasses and blackberries. Male deer grow new antlers every spring, and fawns are born between April and November. Called mule deer because of their large ears, these animals don't run so much as bound, sometimes straight up and down the hillside. Other animals in the hills include *Canis latrans*, or coyote; *Procyon lotor*, the raccoon; the State Bird, the California Valley Quail; jackrabbits; rattlesnakes; bats; and owls. The town's eponymous mountain lions are rarely sighted close to town anymore, but they do inhabit the Santa Cruz Mountains, as do the Black Bears with which Mountain Charley wrestled in the 19th century.

Deer carry ticks, tiny parasites that can transmit disease. Hikers are advised to wear light-colored clothing to make the dark insects easier to see and to cover up with long-sleeved shirts, long pants and hats. Some trekkers duct tape their pants to their socks.

EXPLORING THE SIERRA AZUL is easy thanks to two intersecting trail systems. The Jones Road trail begins at the end of Jones Road, off College Avenue, and leads to Lexington Reservoir. The Kennedy Trail heads south from the top of Kennedy Road at Top of Hill Road and eventually connects with Limekiln and Priest Rock trails, both of which return to Lexington. The trails are open from dawn to dusk. Dogs on leashes are allowed. Bicyclists must wear helmets and observe a 15 mph (24 kph) speed limit. Smoking, fires and all weapons are prohibited. Bring sunscreen and drinking water.

128 Modir Estate
16450 Aztec Ridge Drive
Dr. Jamal Modir, **1989-1994**

Dr. Modir's audacious residence is visible from every corner of Los Gatos and commands breathtaking views of Lexington Reservoir to the south and San Francisco to the north. Inspired by the Montezuma Hills development, Dr. Modir's motif might be called Contemporary Aztec. Brutal columns with fitted, outsized lintels blend with clean simple lines. Materials range from raw concrete to polished marble, with very little wood.

AN UNFRAMED PANE OF GLASS forms the front door of the Modir Estate, a comfortable private home which in some aspects could be mistaken for a contemporary museum. The Roman fountain in the foreground celebrates the arrival of guests.

A two-story atrium with full-sized trees (*ficus benjamina* in particular), a laminar waterfall, and a seamless aquarium forms the center of the 12,000 square foot, three-story home. A Roman fountain, which mixes air with the water, defines the entry. Delightful moments are everywhere, from the glass lavatory sink bowl in the guest bathroom which features a spotlight that lights the floor through the splashing water, to the Art Deco dancing figures etched into the glass doors leading to the master suite.

The kitchen enjoys an unbroken view of the valley and San Francisco Bay beyond, with no overhead cabinets. A desk at one end of the kitchen has a sight line over the heads of guests lounging on the u-shaped sectional to the built-in multi-screen television on the far wall. Every bedroom has a balcony.

Dr. Modir doesn't like visible lines. His doors often run from floor to ceiling and he felt compelled to extend the maid's marble shower enclosure all the way up to avoid an unsightly line. "Trim is to cover mistakes," he explains.

NO BARS DIVIDE THE GLASS, and there are few limits on the vista from the Modir's kitchen. Curved window at the left is actually formed by several straight segments.

Most of the Persian surgeon's 48 acres are unspoiled ridgeline, important because the property adjoins the Mid-Peninsula Open Space District and Dr. Modir points out that the lands around his home will, thanks to his project, not become an extension of the Aztec Ridge tract. The landscaping is not yet complete, and the pool, which will create the illusion that the water hangs at the edge of a cliff, has not been built. One reason for the delay: the estate's creative spirit has yet to decide on a location for the helipad.

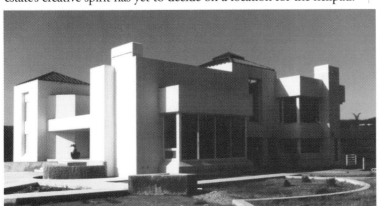

KENNEDY & SHANNON

Kennedy and Shannon Roads head east through the foothills. Observers will not be surprised to learn that the hills were once owned by pioneers Thomas Shannon and James F. Kennedy. Close to town, the property has been developed into gracious tracts such as Longmeadow, while the area farther east is home to large estates such as Casa Milagro and Stonehill.

INDOOR POOL IS A FEW STEPS FROM THE ELEVATOR TO THE MASTER SUITE. Pool and elevator are recent improvements designed by Kenneth Rodrigues and Partners.

129 Elsman House
Address Withheld
c1928

Ralph Elsman, a native of Connecticut, sold his New York electric company and came west in 1925. He invested in the San Jose Water Works, built this impressive estate on Kennedy land in the late 1920s, and became president of San Jose Water in 1937. Over the next thirty years, he masterminded a great expansion which included construction of the dam which created Lake Elsman on Los Gatos Creek near the summit. Originally surrounded by even more acreage, the house still commands a spacious front lawn and beautiful specimen palm trees. The current owners have respected its Mediterranean Revival sensibilities while keeping the home comfortable.

130 Hillbrook School
16000 Marchmont Avenue
c1918

Colonel James S. Parker's ranch at the end of Marchmont Avenue became the Children's Country School in 1936. Called Hillbrook School after 1960, the private academy founded by Miss Mary Oren in 1935 still operates and is currently involved in a multi-year construction project.

Parker bought the home and 38-acre orchard from the Reilly's in 1923 for over $60,000.

• VILLAGE OF FRIENDLY RELATIONS •

STUDENTS BUILT this village with a bank loan and donated materials in the early 1940s during World War II, then sold tea and lemonade to repay the loan. Ten buildings, including the school store and newspaper office were ultimately constructed in what became a school tradition, but only six remain.

143

WITH KNOWING REFERENCE to the wooden sidewalks of East Main Street circa 1885, the Stewart House simultaneously evokes the simple dignity of Peter Johnson's working barn.

LIGHT POURS DOWN from the clerestory cupola into the central hall of the Stewart House. A special exception was found for cupolas in the building code which allowed it to exceed the height limit for the area.

144

131 Stewart House
17105 Phillips Avenue
William Turnbull, Jr., **1997**

Many features of Judge Melinda Stewart's home are unconventional, such as the large sliding panels to hide the kitchen on formal occasions, but other aspects seem thoroughly grounded in an understanding of the vernacular architecture of Northern California. The bifurcated central staircase, the broad front porch, and the board-and-batten siding recall a nineteenth-century saloon. Every detail of the house has been carefully crafted to preserve the historical forms while reminding the observer that a late twentieth-century intellect was at work.

Designed by the world-renowned architect William Turnbull, Jr., FAIA, the house abounds with serendipitous spaces, such as the quiet second floor porch facing the woods, and exquisite details, including the way the simple wooden balustrade disappears into the hardwood floor.

Sadly, the architect died just before the house was completed. Sausalito-based Turnbull (1935-1997) studied at Princeton and the *Ecole de Beaux-Arts* before gaining early notoriety with Charles Moore for their Sea Ranch in 1964. Turnbull's other work includes the 21-room *Inn at Southbridge* near Meadowood in the wine country and an Orinda residence, similar to the Stewart House, which earned him a 1996 AIA California Council Merit Award. Turnbull believed that "architecture should delight the mind, respect the purse and consume the intellect."

Shannon House

132 Shannon House
14475 Shannon Road
c1866

Thomas Shannon (1825-c1900) came to California from Ohio in 1849 seeking gold. Four men died as Shannon's wagon train crossed Death Valley. He acquired this quarter section (160 acres) under the Homestead Act after seven years of paperwork and built this redwood cabin/farmhouse with profits from a lumber business. The house reportedly was a stop on the Los Gatos-Saratoga to Guadalupe-Coyote stagecoach route.

133 Gardner House   🔔 HD-76-4
16230 Shannon Road
Noah Palmer, H. H. Roper (mason),1866

Captain Melvin S. Gardner probably bought the Spring Creek Ranch, some 644 acres surrounding this house, in the late 1870s. His employer, the Knickerbocker Company, sent him to California in 1849, where he made a fortune in mining before settling in Los Gatos. The Spring Creek Ranch, perhaps named for what we now know as Ross Creek, cost him $18,000, or $28 per acre. Such a large sum indicates that the property, which extended from today's Blossom Hill Road to Kennedy and from Los Gatos Boulevard to Short Road, was already quite developed.

In the 1970s, the owner opened the house to the public every Sunday. The house was built in 1866 by Noah Palmer, and bought in 1867 by James F. Payne (for whom Payne Avenue in San Jose is reportedly named). The mason, Henry Horace Roper, signed the chimney in the attic.

THIS EYE-CATCHING DESIGN, an example of recent residential development at 15995 Cerro Vista, boasts a sweeping view, five bedrooms, 4½ bathrooms, a spacious guest house and, in 1998, a $2 million price tag.

Gardner House

145

DESIGNED FOR GRACIOUS LIVING, the Wenzel House juxtaposes light and view against privacy and enclosure. The name, *La Luna*, was inspired by the moonlight which suffuses this hall and adjoining rooms.

146

134 La Luna
16265 Short Road
Kurt B. Anderson, **1993**

A wonderful example of contemporary architecture on a relatively small site, the home of John and Terri Wenzel transforms an otherwise unremarkable residential street. In fact, the new residence was built in the backyard and unveiled with the demolition of the small house in front.

With apparent reference to traditional center hall colonial designs, Kurt Anderson (Andarch Architecture) splits the house down the center with a single-story entertainment wing on the left of the airy central corridor and the rest of the house in a two-story element on the right.

Glass entry doors lead to the fully skylit hall, carrying the eye through the house to the backyard. Even from the street it is possible to look right through the house. Elsewhere, smaller windows and glass block preserve privacy. Gently convex glass block walls refer with a wink to the colonial style's traditional bow window. Make no mistake, however; this house may amuse architects, but it is a practical success on its own terms.

135 Magneson Cottage
16751 Magneson Loop
W. R. Yelland?, **1928**

This may have been Captain Walter C. Magneson's house and it was possibly designed by Berkeley architect W. R. Yelland. Yelland (1890-1966), a native of Los Gatos, is known for other examples of "Hansel & Gretel" architecture in the Bay Area. A passing fashion in the 1920s, the fairy tale style was inspired by Hollywood movie sets. The Little Village shops (see 18) on North Santa Cruz Avenue offer further examples of the style.

The current owners sought the most English house they could find and settled on this one in 1977. The previous owners called the house Carmel Cottage and were slightly eccentric. They had decided, for example, that the house should not suffer an electric refrigerator (the man of the house kept one outdoors in the back-yard for his beer).

Magneson Cottage

FIRST UNITED PRESBYTERIAN CHURCH moved from its original Forbes' mill site to Shannon Road in the late 1950s.
http://www.pclg.org

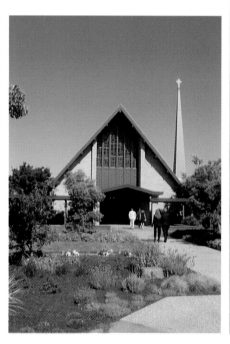

NEW SONG: Congregation Shir Hadash built this new sanctuary, designed by Mark Shatz, in 1996.
http://www.shirhadash.org

147

LOS GATOS BOULEVARD

Until Blossom Hill Road was extended to connect with University and North Santa Cruz in the late 1950s, it ended at Los Gatos Boulevard (then San Jose Avenue). Three large farms traditionally occupied the intersection: Roberts to the west, Cilker to the north and Gardner to the east.

ECHOES OF MUSIC linger on the porch of 315 Los Gatos Boulevard, where friends would gather to play guitar and harmonica and occasionally Yehudi Menuhin would drop by to add his world-famous violin.

The Kennedy-Torrey house at 432 Los Gatos Boulevard

TWO STONE ARCHES create portals into the private garden at the corner of Pine and Los Gatos Boulevard and Pine Avenue. The Craftsman home of Sven and Caroline Sunby features a pyramid roof more often found in earlier Victorians.

136 Thrash House
371 Los Gatos Boulevard
c1916

William and Minnie E. Thrash built the house in the 1910s, and William died between 1925 and 1930. In 1974, the house became administrative offices for the nursing home behind the residence, owned by the National Benevolent Association Health Services Corporation. A fire in 1983 destroyed the first floor, but, in 1985, the town council, based on an appeal by Planning Commissioner Kathryn Morgan, blocked demolition. A standoff ensued, with the undemolishable residence as yet unrestored. Notice the hitching post at the curb.

"GREENE & GREENE WERE MISOGYNISTS," opines Mrs. Berkowitz. The Berkowitz family repaired and restored this gracious Craftsman home following earthquake damage and neglect. They discovered 10" x 10" (25 cm) solid redwood beams under the floor during the renovation. Like the famous Gamble House in Southern California, designed by Charles and Henry Greene, this sprawling bungalow originally featured a sleeping porch. The Greenes practically invented the Craftsman style, but apparently expected only servants in the kitchen. Accordingly, this was the one room that needed modernization.
(Landscaping by Landscape Solutions.)

http://www.calvarylosgatos.org

137 Calvary Baptist Church
16330 Los Gatos Boulevard
Sanctuary: **1953**

The Calvary Baptist Church began when 90 dissenters left the First Baptist Church in 1948. The First congregation had been formed by sixteen Baptists in 1883 and built its first church on West Main Street at Lyndon in 1889. The second church, built in 1917 at College and East Main, resulted from an ideological split dating to 1910.

The current facility, on 7.4 acres, includes a chapel and auditorium on Los Gatos Boulevard, and Brown Hall, a gymnasium and Friesen Hall behind them. Today's church counts 1,800 members and 30 full-time staff. The First Baptist Church, dislocated by the Penthouse Apartments, moved to Farley Road and is now on Daves Avenue in Monte Sereno.

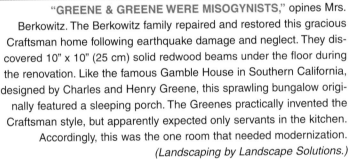
Calvary Baptist Church

Louise Van Meter School

THIS SIMPLE, AUTHENTIC ADOBE structure at 16461 Los Gatos Boulevard survived the 1989 earthquake with only minor cracks, but the contractor needed a trip to the library to learn how to repair adobe.

King's Court Center

http://www.lvm.lgusd.k12.ca.us

138 Louise Van Meter Elementary School
16445 Los Gatos Boulevard
Harry Lincoln, **1948**

One of three elementary schools in Los Gatos, this was the first to be built away from University Avenue. The school is named for Louise Van Meter (1869-1948), the first grade teacher at the University Avenue Grammar School for many years. Miss Van Meter started teaching in Los Gatos in 1893 after four years in the Union District and Pacheco Pass schools, and she was ultimately successful, in 1928, in her decades-long campaign to provide kindergarten for her children.

The school's sensitive design provides north light to most classrooms and brings trees and grass up close, where the children can watch the seasons change.

Van Meter was followed by Daves Avenue School in August, 1953; Blossom Hill Elementary in 1958 and Raymond J. Fisher Middle School in 1961.

A PLEASANT CRAFTSMAN bungalow, 16190 Los Gatos Boulevard is yet another new old design by Chris Spaulding. It is also another example of "mixed-use" with apartments above offices.

139 King's Court Center
700-798 Blossom Hill Road
1960, 1963

King's Court is one of the town's oldest suburban shopping centers, built on a small corner of Captain Gardner's Spring Creek Ranch which once extended south to Kennedy and east to Short Road.

A second phase, built in 1963, added a Safeway market (which is now Lunardi's) and an un-built third phase was to have included a department store.

Blossom Hill Center

140 Blossom Hill Pavilion
624-640 Blossom Hill Road
Kenneth Rodrigues & Partners, **1996**

The Blossom Hill Pavilion (formerly the Byer Center) is typical of recent commercial architecture anywhere in the United States. Designed for faux quaintness and anything—literally, anything—to avoid being one big box, the Pavilion became controversial during construction specifically for its 36' (11m) dome, rather than for its studied lack of architectural honesty. The design fits more than a half acre of retail floor space onto a two-acre site. Perhaps the pointless façades are meant to evoke the commercial architecture of the Old West, and the useless dome, porch and doors-to-nowhere are homage to Sarah Winchester's famous mystery house.

Ironically, the building is constructed of high quality materials and was designed by the same San Jose firm that created the far more architecturally successful Cornerstone center across the street.

141 Cornerstone
15920-15996 Los Gatos Boulevard
Kenneth Rodrigues & Partners (Peter Ko), **1992-94**

Prune and apricot orchards, long in the Cilker family, became a suburban retail center in 1961, as other orchards in the area, notably Blossom Manor, became tracts of houses. In 1992, Cilker Orchards decided to renovate and improve the aging center, just as the Town of Los Gatos sponsored a community

Cornerstone

151

Cornerstone Retail Center

"charette" (an intensive design session) focusing on the urban planning of Los Gatos Boulevard. The result of Elizabeth Cilker Smith's involvement with the charette is that the corner became a "node" in the overall design for the boulevard.

Cornerstone is a 51,782 square foot retail complex featuring paired white columns, symmetrical penetrations and fenestration, a corner tower and an articulated façade. Elizabeth Smith explains that the first designs proposed a block of dark, western-style storefronts. Instead, a more refined style was chosen that attempts a Yankee ambience based on the observation that antique Los Gatos designs were often East Coast transplants. The round, copper-roofed tower pays homage to downtown's signature La Cañada Building.

The Cilker family has a long history in Los Gatos. In 1886, John Cilker, owner of 174 acres near today's Highway 85, founded the Co-Operative Winery on land now occupied by the Civic Center. Arch Cilker was a director of the First National Bank during the Great Depression, and the family sold and donated land for the Good Samaritan hospital.

Yuki Farms

http://www.northlosgatos.com

142 Yuki Farms
Los Gatos Boulevard and Lark Avenue

As the last remaining large parcel in town, the zoning of Yuki Farms' 40-acre walnut orchard at the intersection of highways 17 and 85 has received considerable attention in recent years. The town council's grassroots General Plan Task Force debated the property's future at length.

When Highway 85 was constructed, some assumed that a regional mall made sense at the off-ramps. So-called "big box retail," such as Wal-Mart or Home Depot is another possibility. Many, however, would like to see the orchard remain as a monument to Los Gatos' agrarian tradition. For now, there are no plans to develop the bulk of the property.

VINELAND & FARM LANDS

Before tracts and street trees obscured the view, the broad valley spread to the horizon to the north and east of town. Heading toward San Jose on what became Los Gatos Boulevard, a traveler at the turn of the century would come to Vineland at the intersection with the road to Almaden. Justice of the Peace and Town Recorder Eben Farley had an 18 acre orchard in Vineland and the tiny locale was centered on today's Farley Road. (Vineland Avenue, on the west side of the creek, aligns more or less with Farley.)

Heading east, the farms of San Jose's southern Union District come into view, bounded on the south by the northernmost foothill in the Sierra Azul, a pristine rise, covered in spring with flowers and budding trees, known as Blossom Hill.

In 1890, Frank Hamilton owned two hundred acres of this land including the northern slope of Blossom Hill, near today's Union Avenue. The Hamilton farmhouse survived, more or less, for over a hundred years, as the orchards were replaced, little by little, by homes and shopping centers. In 1999, the Summerhill Homes project replaced the second-to-last large orchard remaining in Los Gatos.

GOOD SAMARITAN HOSPITAL, or Good Sam as it is known, is just outside the town's northern boundary. The venerable oak tree on the left, here perhaps 100 years before the hospital, is the facility's symbol. The six-story building opened in 1965 and was bought by Columbia/HCA in January 1996 along with three other area hospitals.

http://www.retirementlife.com/terraces.html

143 The Terraces of Los Gatos
800 Blossom Hill Road
Stone, Marraccini & Patterson, **1992-93**

About 300 seniors live in The Terraces, built on an 8.9-acre walnut orchard after nearly eight years of political debate. The nonprofit American Baptist Homes of the West built and operates the facility, which features a variety of living situations. There are some 175 independent units, 35 assisted living and 59 skilled nursing units. Residents pay $109,000 or more for the right to pay $1,767 and up in monthly fees, and the waiting list attests to the project's success as a residential community.

The Terraces

Hoerler House

144 Hoerler House
15945 Camino del Cerro
c1877

HD-84-1

A nicely restored two-story vernacular Victorian farm house, built by a Pennsylvania Dutchman named Hoerler. Unlike more overt gambrel barn shapes in town, the Hoerler House's unusually deep cantilevered eave and a clipped gable merely suggest a Pennsylvania Dutch barn.

The house was surrounded at one time by 500 acres of fruit trees. Hoerler's eight sons were born in this house and their initials are reportedly carved in the porch columns. The semi-circular living room was added in 1895.

Vote House

145 A. C. Vote House
16780 Farley Road
c1887

A. C. Vote owned this classic vernacular Queen Anne farmhouse in 1888 when it sat opposite the Vineland School, which was moved to 269 Los Gatos Boulevard in 1905 (see 68).

The restoration of the house, which sits on a quarter acre and includes a carriage house with a hay loft, won a Bellringer award in 1987. The house was raised and a concrete foundation poured just in time to help the centenarian survive the 1989 earthquake.

FUTURE HOMES will be built on this large property approaching the eastern town boundary on Blossom Hill Road near Union Avenue. Summerhill Homes won the right to develop the property, which was bequeathed to the University of California, after years of neighborhood meetings, public hearings and donation of perpetual open space. Summerhill's patient attitude is considered a model by the Planning Department.

Pratt House

FUTURE QUAINT Craftsman-style homes built in 1997 at 101-161 Serra Court (Roberts and Blossom Hill) on the site of a red-wood frame house built by Michael Schmitt in 1895. The impressive stone retaining walls facing Blossom Hill Road seem stark today, but they echo similar walls on Pennsylvania, Alpine and elsewhere in town and they are sure to mature gracefully.

146 Pratt House
HD-75-7

16920 Farley Road
c**1849** (original cabin)

One of the oldest home sites in the area, this house overlooked the Hernandez adobe (in today's Vasona Park, near the Billy Jones railroad). It was originally a cabin, likely built by a squatter hoping to lay claim to the land, dating to the late 1840s. The United States took possession of California from Mexico at that time, leading to much confusion over land records. By the 1860s, J. W. McMillan, one of the new owners of Forbes Mill, owned and probably improved the cabin. As late as 1939, however, the house had no running water, electricity, gas, telephone or sewer.

Eugene L. Pratt (c1856-1939) bought the house and 110 acres surrounding it in the 1880s. Eugene was a Southern Pacific Railroad engineer and orchardist. The freeway unfortunately separates the house from its former acreage at Vasona, but the now much-smaller property is still lovely, with several beautiful trees and a red barn on the Frank Avenue side.

Pratt barn

147 Noah Rogers House

16351 Los Gatos-Almaden Road
c1883

HD-78-2

One of the more unusual historic residences in town, set behind wrought iron and a blacktop turnaround off the busy Los Gatos-Almaden Road. The old house is just one of the oddities on display, as the current owners have collected street clocks, a windmill and other assorted artifacts.

Noah Garcelon Rogers, a fruit rancher, purchased the house in 1888 as part of a 270-acre ranch which extended from the Los Gatos Cemetery to the San Jose Road (now Los Gatos Boulevard). Rogers operated the Los Gatos Cured Fruit Company, which had its three-story packing house at the intersection of San Jose and Almaden Roads.

NEIGHBORS SINCE 1888:
Downing Center.

148 Downing Center

15525-15569 Union Avenue

An inviting suburban shopping center on the eastern edge of town, built on the Downing farm in the early 1960s, about the same time that the Gardner and Cilker orchards became retail centers on San Jose Road. A sign labels Downing "neighbors since 1888."

A one-of-a-kind fountain stands just south of the supermarket. It consists of a large water tank suspended in a modern tower, allowed to drip continuously.

OAK MEADOW

The Los Gatos Creek Trail winds through a leafy paradise known as Oak Meadow and passes under Roberts Road and Blossom Hill Road before reaching the town's Oak Meadow Park, next door to the county's Vasona Park. The roads around the park have changed since the 1950s. University Avenue from Blossom Hill to Lark was the railroad alignment. Blossom Hill Road did not connect to North Santa Cruz Avenue until the early 1960s.

The location of the town park was formerly the town dump. When freeway construction destroyed Memorial Park south of the Main Street Bridge (accessed by Park Avenue, which still remains), the dump was purchased as a replacement.

NARROW CONCRETE BRIDGE on Roberts Road was built in 1903 at the request of James and Catherine Forrest.

Los Gatos Creek Trail at Oak Meadow

149 Nino House
129 Ohlone Court

Sofia and Graziano Nino arrived from Italy in 1882 and bought this property from John J. Roberts the following year. The Ninos had six children, among them Edward and Albert, interviewed by town historian William Wulf in 1978. Graziano died in 1904 and Sofia was left to raise the children alone.

Nino House

Forrest House, Merry Oaks

150 Merry Oaks
120 Oak Meadow
1889-90

This dignified house, now surrounded by development, with the road at its very doorstep, was the home of James Morgan Forrest and his wife Catherine. James came to California from Boston in the late 1850s. On October 29, 1889, the Forrests bought six acres from John J. Roberts. Forrest and his son first practiced their building skills on a barn, and next, using designs prepared by Catherine and James, built the family home, with the help of an experienced carpenter.

We know so much about the Forrests because their daughter, Carrie Forrest Wells, wrote a series of reminiscences for the newspaper from 1939 to 1943. The home fell into disrepair in the early 1970s and by 1976 it housed the Center for Human Communication, a therapy group.

The current owners, who call the house *Merry Oaks*, have made it a showplace, earning a Bellringer award in 1987. The much smaller property still contains eleven oak trees.

OPEN 8 A.M. to sunset. Dogs on leashes allowed. Fee parking.

151 Oak Meadow Park
250 Blossom Hill Road
McDonald H. Smith (landscape architect), **1958**

Oak Meadow replaced the town's beloved Memorial Park (located south of the Main Street bridge) which fell victim to Highway 17's construction in 1954. Twelve acres that had served as a dump were purchased from Mr. and Mrs. Pietro Denevi and a grassroots Development Committee was formed in the mid 1950s. The committee approved Smith's master plan, which included the large open lawn that he called "Grand Meadow," in April 1958.

From its inception, the town's park has benefited from thousands of volunteer hours and donated services. The Billy Jones Wildcat Railroad was established here after about ten years, and the carousel was restored twenty years after that. The playground features a T33A training jet on loan from the U. S. Air Force and a La France fire engine, retired when the town joined the Central Fire District in 1970.

Billy Jones Wildcat Railroad

William Jones (1884-1968) was a life-long live steam enthusiast who began working on the Southern Pacific Railroad at age 13 as a roustabout and worked his way to engineer by age 21. In 1917, he bought a nine-acre ranch (at Winchester and Daves Avenue, marked today by a plaque) and married Geraldine McGrady, a school marm from the Santa Cruz Mountains. Of their four children, both boys were killed in World War II. Starting at age 57, in 1941, and for the next six years, Billy Jones built a 1/3-scale railroad around his prune orchard and welcomed children and other visitors, including Walt Disney.

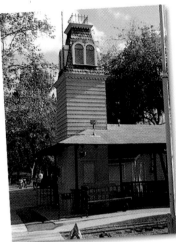

Disney reportedly made an offer for "Old No. 2," the 2-6-2 locomotive that Jones had purchased from the Venice, California Overfair Railroad. Jones turned Walt down, but Disney didn't leave empty-handed: Los Gatan Joe Fowler, a retired admiral, agreed to head south "temporarily" to manage Disneyland's 1954 construction and ended up serving as the park's general manager for the next dozen years.

APRIL THROUGH OCTOBER, tickets for the mile-long BJWRR can be purchased at the depot, designed in 1970 by Higgins and Root.

After Jones' death, volunteers led by local electrician Bill Mason moved the train and its five-ton locomotive to Oak Meadow. A golden spike was driven on July 26, 1970, and in 1972 the track was extended by 3,500 feet (1067 m) into neighboring Vasona Park. Some 70,000 passengers each year ride the nearly mile-long (1.6 km) loop.

BJWRR Vasona Trestle

Notice the two bridges: The forty foot (12 m) curved trestle was designed and built by volunteer railfans, but the 86-foot (26.2 m) span over Los Gatos Creek (just outside the depot) is actually a salvaged Southern Pacific piggyback flat car. Another point of interest: The BJWRR initially shut down at 5:27 p. m. each day to commemorate the time of the last Southern Pacific train through Los Gatos on January 25, 1959.

William E. Mason Carousel

The carousel, named for the man who led the Billy Jones railroad volunteers, opened in 1991 after ten years of restoration work. Original built circa 1910 by the Frederick Savage Company of England, the makers of the first steam roundabouts in the 1860s, it traveled through the Panama canal to participate in the 1915 Panama-Pacific Exhibition. As refurbished, the clockwise carousel features 30 horses, including some carved by C. J. Parker, Dare, and Armitage-Herschel.

W. E. Mason Carousel   **159**

OPEN 8 A.M. to one half hour after sunset. Dogs on leashes allowed. Beer and wine with picnic meals only.

UNMARKED, the Hernandez adobe site had a view of Mt. Umunhum and today lies within the tracks of the BJWRR.

Vasona's ducks are in a row.

152 Vasona Lake County Park
Blossom Hill Road & Highway 17 (298 Garden Hill Drive)
1961

Vasona is a beautiful 151-acre park surrounding the 57-acre lake created by damming Los Gatos Creek in the 1950s. The large playground is surrounded by various picnic areas. Six miles of paved pathways include a segment of the Los Gatos Creek Trail, which extends from Willow Glen to Lexington Reservoir's Lenihan Dam. Wildlife of all kinds, particularly ducks, enjoy the water and the natural surroundings.

Vasona is adjacent to the town's Oak Meadow Park and the tracks of the volunteer-built Billy Jones Wildcat Railroad loop through the larger county park. The site of Jose Hernandez' 1839 adobe home lies, unmarked, inside the loop on the high ground just east of the creek.

The park is named for the nearby Vasona Junction, the point at which the railroad to Los Gatos branched off toward Saratoga. Reportedly, it became a regular stop in the 1890s simply for the convenience of a local farmer's daughter who worked in town. The stop needed a name, and the farmer recalled a favorite pony named Vasona from his youth.

The Youth Science Institute, founded at Alum Rock Park in 1953, opened a branch at Vasona in 1980. A third facility, at Sanborn Park in the Santa Cruz Mountains, opened in 1982. YSI offers programs and classes for children from preschool through elementary school and Science Safaris for families. Programs include the "Four Senses Nature Walk," "Earthquake Walk," and "Bat Hikes," conducted at night. Every January, the institute sponsors a Whale Watch.

NORTHSIDE

North of downtown and south of Oak Meadow lies a Los Gatos neighborhood that we have arbitrarily named Northside. Some say the area is an extension of other neighborhoods, but Highway 9 is an unmistakable boundary.

THE BLOCK MASSING of this bank at 449 North Santa Cruz Avenue, designed in 1980 by Lawrence Simons & Associates, has been mellowed by ivy over the years, but landscaping does not hide its pleasant juxtaposition of form, color and material. The exuberant trelliswork along the front seems to interpret Victorian filigree and the human scale of the intersecting blocks is reminiscent of Frank Lloyd Wright's Fallingwater.

153 Puccinelli Dehydrating Company
565 University Avenue
1921, 1928, 1961, Renovation: Kenneth Rodrigues **1996**

The barns on this site were built in 1921 by Romolo L. Puccinelli. It was here that Puccinelli perfected his technique for drying fruit, and in 1928 he expanded into the current building, drying fruit as well as manufacturing dehydration equipment.

In 1961, partners who had worked together at Sterling Lumber on University Avenue near Main Street, remodeled the old barn into El Gato Building Materials. The current 11,000 square foot facility is a new reconstruction of the original. Campo di Bocce means, simply, "bocce village," and describes a bocce ball club and restaurant which opened in February 1997. Certainly a unique environment, with bocce ball games surrounding fine dining, the interior features a mural by John Espinola.

BELLRINGER REMODEL at 441 San Benito Avenue features miniature carriage doors and charming trellis work.

161

154 Place d'Anderegg
510-550 Monterey Avenue
Ray and Sharon Anderegg, Fosco Piva (mason), c1980

One of the first multi-family residential projects to employ French Norman style in the area, the *Place d' Anderegg* showcases the work of fine builder Ray Anderegg and master brickmason Fosco Piva.

The brick walls, chimneys and accents are a virtual patternbook for those planning brick projects. Piva, continuing a long tradition of Italian masonry in town which includes Quintino Ceccanti and the wall at College Avenue and Main Street, made the project a tour de force. For example, each of five brick patios features a different pattern.

WALK TO TOWN, NORTH, includes some interesting vintage homes. This house, at 425 University, illustrates the vaguely sinister winter mood that Victorian homes can project before they are prettied up and made spring-like again.

NORTHERN ENVIRONS

The north and west edges of town, orchards and farms until the 1950s, include several modern tracts. In 1994, Highway 85, planned in the 1960s, was completed, cutting a swath through the upper corner of the town.

The intersection of Quito Road and Saratoga Road in Monte Sereno was once a little community called Austin Corners, but today it would be a distraction to the drivers zooming between Los Gatos and Saratoga. The electric interurban trolley came to Los Gatos along this road until 1933, with stops at Nippon Mura (now La Hacienda Inn), Austin Corners, and Daves Avenue before turning to travel the length of North Santa Cruz Avenue.

LOADED WITH AMENITIES because the Town of Los Gatos would not have approved of "big box retail" otherwise, the Office Depot at 15166 Los Gatos Boulevard (Mark Thieme, 1995) features a clock, a fountain, display windows, a columned arcade and a mini-park (a boulevard "node") which are rarely, if ever, used. It is a pleasant architectural experience nonetheless, and it anticipates future retail at this end of the boulevard.

http://207.70.79.108/cheo/docs/Los_Gatos_Lodge.html

 155 Elks Lodge
105 Newell Avenue (at Winchester Boulevard)
Gifford Sobey, **1966**

The Benevolent Paternal Order of Elks, Los Gatos Lodge (No. 1857), founded in 1952, commissioned this cantilevered headquarters from local architect and Elk Gifford Sobey in 1966.

An American social club, as opposed to an international service organization such as the Lions, the B. P. O. E. is particularly proud of its many members who fought for their country in the 20th century.

BILLY JONES' 9-acre prune ranch at Daves Avenue and Winchester is remembered by this plaque.

Courtside

156 Courtside Club
14675 Winchester Boulevard
A. C. Martin, **1976**
DES Architecture + Engineering,**1998**

Originally a tennis club, Courtside has recently remodeled as a "sports resort," with many innovative family-oriented programs. The current club includes 15 outdoor and four indoor tennis courts, two exercise studios and a 75-foot (23m) pool. The facility includes luxurious locker rooms, a pro shop and offers massage, facials, pedicures and personal fitness training.

157 Simond Adobe
14610 Quito Road
c1854

HD-67-6

Once thought to have been either the Hernandez or Peralta adobe, the original house on this site was actually constructed by Claude Simond, a French raiser of sheep. Monsieur Simond purchased the western third of the Rancho Rinconada de Los Gatos from Sebastian Peralta on January 18, 1853 for $2,500. He called his ranch Rancho Rinconera (the little corner).

Tragically, Simond was severely burned aboard the steamboat Jenny Lind when it exploded in San Francisco Bay a few months later. Unable to manage his land, he went bankrupt and creditor Edward Auzerais acquired the house and land April 10, 1857. Auzerais subdivided the property and the house was eventually bought by the wife of the youngest son of José Hernandez, the other original ranchero, leading to the modern misunderstanding about the house's builder.

The current house, set on two acres, is several steps removed from the original, but still contains some adobe walls from the original abode built in the 1850s.

Simond Adobe

158 La Rinconada Country Club
14595 Clearview Drive
1929 Renovation: **1989**

La Rinconada is a private golf club limited to 401 members which anchors the surrounding residential community in a mode that was popular in the 1950s and 1960s. The course and the tasteful clubhouse offer surpisingly spectacular views. The club was dedicated by State Senator Sanborn Young, a founding vice president, on June 2, 1929. The membership has included Bank of America founders A. P. Giannini and James Bacigalupi.

COUNTRY CLUB LIVING awaits in Rancho Rinconada, an upscale development built in the late 1960s surrounding La Rinconada, an exclusive golf club. Golfers are warned (by tips found on the Internet) that the lake on the 306-yard (280m) 14th hole wants an iron, not a driver, and that the par-5 18th hole is perhaps too easy.

Golf Links Avenue

159 Open Doors
634 West Parr Avenue
Hooper, Olmsted & Hrovat, **1992**

Open Doors. Terra Media (landscape architects)

As part of its commitment to affordable housing, the Town of Los Gatos encourages development of Below Market Price (BMP) residential units, and Open Doors, built by Mid-Peninsula Housing, is that strategy's most prominent success. The 64 apartments at Open Doors are attractive, coordinated yet individual, and feature shared amenities. The complex, which only rents to families, has centrally located play equipment and a Child Development Center (daycare) on site.

We conclude our observation of Los Gatos with Open Doors because we hope it represents the spirit of the town in the new millenium: High quality, purposeful and inclusionary.

165

The Forbes Mill Footbridge Youth Mural

The illustrations in Chapter Two are by local artists of a variety of ages, taken from the Forbes Mill Footbridge Youth Mural. The footbridge is publicly accessible from the Forbes Mill parking lot and from the rear of Old Town.

COMMITTEE CHAIRS
Cynthia Rostankowski
Carol Taylor
Carol Ann Weber

VOLUNTEERS
Bruce Baker
Pat Dryan
Amy Konsterlie
Anne Lamborn
Alice Lopes
Pat Murphy
Phil Seaton
Carole Shaver
Jim Sugai
Wendy Vanni

SPECIAL THANKS
Joanne Benjamin - Roger Poyner
Los Gatos Art Supplies
St. Luke's Episcopal Church
Los Gatos Coffee Roasting Company

MADE POSSIBLE BY
The Town of Los Gatos
Old Town/Hunter Properties
Arts Council of Santa Clara County
Kiwanis and Optimists of Los Gatos
T. K. Construction

Appendices

A Town Parks

B Origins of Place Names

C Mayors

D Bibliography

Blossom Hill Park

A Town Parks

	Size (Acres)	Playground	Picnic Tables	Restrooms	Basketball	Tennis	Baseball	Volleyball	Nature Trails	Bike Path
Bachman Belmont & Bachman	3.6	X	X		X					
Belgatos Belgatos Road	7.4	X	X	X						
Blossom Hill Blossom Hill, Shannon Road	9.2	X	X	X		6	X			
Corporation Yard Miles Avenue				X			X			
Fairview Plaza Fairview Plaza										
Howes Playlot Union at Howes	.5	X								
La Rinconada Wedgewood & Granada	14	X	X			1				
Live Oak Manor Gateway Dr. & Carlton	4.09	X			X			X		
Los Gatos Creek Trail Lexington to Vasona									X	X
Novitiate Park End of Jones Road	8								X	X

	Size (Acres)	Playground	Picnic Tables	Restrooms	Basketball	Tennis	Baseball	Volleyball	Nature Trails	Bike Path
Oak Hill Playlot Garden Lane and Oak Park Dr	.25	X								
Oak Meadow Blossom Hill Road	12	X	X	X					X	
Pageant Grounds South of Civic Center										
Town Plaza Main & Santa Cruz Avenue										
Worcester Worcester Loop	11.2								X	

B Origins of Place Names

Alberto Way. Apparently named for Colonel Alberto Merrill (known as A. E. to most), mayor 1954-1962.

Alexander Avenue. Unknown. Developed by Ellen and A. C. Short, so it is likely that Mr. Short's first name was Alexander. (Ellen gave her name to Ellenwood Avenue, which crosses.) Possibly for William G. Alexander, a member of the Los Gatos Real Estate and Building Association c. 1890.

Almendra Avenue. From the Spanish *almendra*, almond, as in Almond Grove. The 1895 Town Directory lists an Almond Avenue intersecting Massol.

Alpine Avenue. Reportedly named, perhaps by German A. Hildebrand, to entice German tourists from San Francisco to the bucolic hinterlands of Los Gatos.

Altura Vista. Spanish meaning view of elevated ground, literally, height view.

Apricot Lane. Likely for the fruit trees.

Aztec Ridge Drive. The main street of the Montezuma Hills development. Montezuma was the chief of the Aztecs when Cortez arrived in the New World.

Bachman Avenue. Benjamin Franklin Bachman, farmer of 50 acres including today's Glen Ridge, with 32 acres planted to fruit trees, after his arrival in 1880.

Bacigalupi Court. Named for James A. Bacigalupi, first president of the Bank of America.

Bayview Avenue. Likely in reference to an imaginary view of San Francisco Bay, the road intersected West Main on the 1895 Sanborn map, but did not yet connect with Bean to the north.

Bean Avenue. John Bean, retired Michigan manufacturer, inventor of his patented Spray Pump, and founder of the Mountain Spring Water Company, which operated a pump house where Bean Avenue meets the rise known as Glen Ridge.

Bella Vista Avenue. Spanish for "beautiful view," it was named circa 1910. *See also* "Fairview Plaza."

Belmont Avenue. Unknown. The city of Belmont (San Mateo County) was established in 1850, taking its name from the Italian *bel monte*, "beautiful mountain."

Blossom Hill Road. Blossom Hill, 907 feet (277 m) above sea level is just south of this road, west of Union Avenue. The Santa Clara Valley, known as the Valley of Heart's Delight, was a dazzling spectacle in spring when thousands of acres of fruit trees blossomed.

Blossom Manor. The Blossom Manor development (c.1960) named its streets for local plants: Almond Blossom, Apple Blossom, Azalea, Camelia, Cherry Blossom, Cherrystone, Dahlia, Escobar, Gardenia, Jacaranda, Jasmine, Lavender, Lilac, Oleander, Orange Blossom, Roseleaf.

Broadway. Traditional name for a grand, important street. Named by John W. Lyndon for his subdivision, one of the first in the area.

Brooklyn Avenue. Formerly a street, now incorporated into the high school off Pleasant. See also Chicago and New York.

Camino del Cerro. Road of the hill/back of an animal. *See* Cerro Vista.

Camino del Sol. Road of the sun.

Central Avenue. Unknown. The street follows a ridge line roughly halfway between the creek and the hill (El Monte) at the east end of Main Street.

Cerro Chico. Small, or young, hill.

Cerro Vista. The Spanish word *cerro* means hill, or an animal's back. Here, likely a reference to Blossom Hill.

Charles Street. Unknown. Likely named for someone's first or last name.

171

Chestnut Avenue. Subdivided by the McCullaghs, and so likely a reference either to a street or district in Philadelphia or to the trees (*Castanea dentata*) mostly native to the east coast.

Chicago Avenue. Formerly a street, now incorporated into the high school property. See also Brooklyn and New York.

Church Street (formerly Mill Street). The road to Forbes Mill became better known for the Presbyterian and Methodist churches.

Cleland Avenue. William Cleland, developer of the area south of today's civic center.

Clifton Avenue. Origin unknown. The upper end of Broadway is referred to as "Clifton Mound" in 1887.

College Avenue (formerly Wilcox). Refers to the Sacred Heart Novitiate, once a college (seminary) for priests. The college property was purchased in 1887 from Harvey Wilcox.

Creffield Heights. Named for Ralph Creffield, an early land owner.

Cross Way (formerly Wright). Named for the subdivider, Anna Cross (and not, as might be assumed, because it cuts across from Loma Alta to Johnson).

Cypress Way. Unknown. Cypress trees (genus *Cupressus*) are not native to the Bay Area, and yet Oakland has a Cypress freeway and Los Gatos has Cypress Way.

Daves Avenue. John E. Daves, farmer of over 500 acres in Saratoga, arrived in the area from Illinois in 1852. Various members of the Daves family owned property and were prominent citizens at and before the turn of the century.

DiDuca Way. Probably for Mark DiDuca, mayor 1973.

Dittos Lane. Edward Ditto, owner of a one acre orchard in the 1887 town directory.

Edelen Avenue. Mr. Edelen (first name unknown) subdivided the area with his friend, John Miles in 1886. Formerly known as The Vineyard, the area was bounded by University Avenue (then School Street) to the west, the creek to the east, the school to the south and the spur railroad track leading to Forbes Mill on the north.

Ellenwood Avenue. Subdivided by Ellen Short, wife of Glen Ridge developer A. C. Short.

El Cajón Way. Spanish for "the big box," which can mean box canyon, drawer, horse stall, or muddle-headed person.

El Sombroso. Reportedly intended to mean "The Nightwatchman" by well-meaning civic boosters acting in the 1920s to give the town more romance. *See also* Monte Sereno.

Fairview Plaza. Frank McCullagh's subdivision of the early 1880s on the hill at the end of West Main Street. Due to its elevation, the knoll commanded a fair view.

Farley Road. Judge Ebenezer C. Farley. Listed as a farmer of 18 acres near today's road in the 1887 town directory. The 1902 directory lists Eben as a Justice of the Peace, Town Recorder and cashier (officer) of the Bank of Los Gatos.

Fiesta Way (formerly Grays, formerly LaMontaigne). The *Fiesta de Los Gatos* supplanted the annual pageant beginning in 1957 and served as the forerunner to today's annual *Fiesta de* [los] *Artes*.

Fisher Avenue. Named for the middle school built in 1960 named for Raymond J. Fisher, elementary school principal (1928-59).

Foster Road. Vincent and Sarah Foster owned 160 acres here at one time, a portion of which he bought from his father Isaac in 1853. The road is officially Foster/Verser because the Fosters granted a right-of-way easement to Francis Verser, who owned the south face of St. Joseph's Hill in the latter 19th century.

Garden Hill Drive. Unknown. Blossom Hill Road was extended through Vasona in the early 1960s. Perhaps this name continues the Blossom Hill tradition.

Glenridge Avenue. The Glen Ridge Park tract was subdivided just after the turn of the century by A. C. Short. There is some confusion whether the name was once two words: "Glen Ridge," as an extant concrete curb is stamped, but it is a single word today, probably an efficiency of the post office. Glen is a Celtic term for "narrow valley," which is not accurate topologically, but it is a very popular real estate name. (Glenwood, near Santa Cruz, was established prior to 1880.) The block connecting Pennsylvania and Hernandez was known as Taylor Street, for the Alameda family which owned several lots, but was officially changed in 1909.

Gray's Lane. Not certain, but a Mrs. Z. E. Gray owned the Los Gatos Home School in the 1887 town directory. Fiesta Way was once called Gray's Lane, and the name was transferred (probably in 1965) to avoid being lost.

Grove Street. No doubt in reference to the acres of fruit orchards visible from the street in the early 20th century.

Happy Acres Road. Named for the subdivision, Happy Acres. No further information.

Harding Avenue. Probably named for Warren G. Harding, 29th president, who died in San Francisco, August 2, 1923.

Hernandez Avenue. Romantically named at or after the turn of the century for José Maria Hernandez, co-grantee of the original rancho. Hernandez and his brother-in-law Peralta profited little from their grant and both were dead when streets were named in their honor.

Hicks Road. Probably named for the lands of J. A. Hicks, town trustee (councilmember) 1893-94.

Highland Avenue. Many streets in town are named for the view that their increased elevation affords.

High School Court. Created when the high school moved from University Avenue to a new campus off East Main Street in 1908.

Hilow Road. Unknown.

Jackson Street. Frank M. Jackson, one of the committee of 13 that determined the town's boundaries in 1887. Listed as Postmaster and stationer in the 1887 Town Directory and served as trustee (councilman) 1890-92.

Johnson Avenue. Subdivided by Peter Johnson, a teamster, farmer and provisioner in the early 1880s. Member of Board of Trustees (councilman) 1888-94, chairman (mayor) 1892-94.

Jones Road. Zachariah "Buffalo" Jones, owner of the mill at Lexington in the 1850s, built this road to carry lumber to market. The original road continues after the paving stops as a biking and hiking trail.

Kennedy Road. James F. Kennedy, toll collector on the Santa Cruz Gap Turnpike toll road (1857-77).

Kimble Avenue. Named for Mr. Kimble, an early landowner in the foothills northeast of the Novitiate.

Knowles Drive. Pollard Road extension named in 1977 to honor early town physician Dr. Frank W. Knowles (1858-c1944), at the instigation of history-minded mayor Mardi Gualtieri Bennett.

La Estancia. The McCullagh estate, reportedly named by Mary McCullagh. The Spanish *estancia* means stay, or visit, but the meaning in South America is ranch. The McCullaghs returned to their original Philadelphia at one point, but returned to make their home here.

La Rinconada. The name of the original Hernandez-Peralta grant was La Rinconada de los Gatos, the corner of the cats. *Rinconada* means external corner, such as an intersection, while *rincón* refers to an internal corner, or nook. Unlike some names borrowed from Spanish, here the gender matches and modern pronunciation is correct.

Lark Avenue. Unknown, perhaps in reference to the meadowlark (*Alaudidae Sturnella*), or possibly a surname.

Las Astas, Flores, Miradas. Spanish for the horns, the flowers and the looks or glances. All apparent references to bullfighting.

Laurel Drive. Likely named for the native tree (*Laurus nobilis*).

Loma Alta Avenue (formerly Market Street). Subdivider Peter Johnson named the road Market Street somewhat hopefully in the early 1880s, but it never became a commercial center due to its distance from the train depot. In February 1921, the town council acted on a petition from the residents and changed the name to Loma Alta, high land/ridge.

Los Cerritos Drive. Spanish for the little hills.

Los Gatos Boulevard (formerly San Jose Avenue). The road to San Jose had been, logically, San Jose Road, as long as settlers have been here (i.e., since the late 1830s). In the 1920s it became the more genteel San Jose Avenue, and with the race to annex suburbia in full swing during the 1950s, the town claimed the road for its own citizens through the expedient of a name change.

Los Gatos-Almaden Road. Inter-urban roads in this area have traditionally been named for their terminal towns, often with the names reversed at each end. (That is, in Almaden the road might be known as Almaden-Los Gatos Road.) Thus, Los Gatos-Saratoga Road (which becomes Saratoga-Sunnyvale Road at Saratoga). This nomenclature is somewhat cumbersome and is occasionally shortened: for example, the Campbell-Almaden Road is known as Camden.

Los Robles Way. Spanish for the oaks, referring to deciduous oaks, rather than *encinas*, or Coast Live Oak.

Lundy Lane. It is recorded that a Mr. Lundy was the first subscriber of the town's first newspaper, the *News*, in 1881.

Lyndon Avenue, Plaza. West Main Street (and other streets, particularly Broadway) was developed by John Weldon Lyndon, owner of the Los Gatos Hotel, where Lyndon Plaza stands today. His brother James was also a prominent citizen.

Madrone Avenue. Likely named for the native tree (*Arbutus menziesii*), derived from the Spanish *madroño*.

Magenson Loop. Captain Walter C. Magneson, subdivider of the area. The road "loops" to connect Los Gatos Boulevard with Shannon Road.

Main Street. Originally, as in most towns, the title of "main" street was quite literal. In our case, the only official street in town for some years (1850 until the mid-1870s) led to the bridge across Los Gatos Creek, in nearly the same location as today's bridge across Highway 17. East Main Street is east of the bridge and West Main is west.

Marchmont Drive. Unknown.

Maricopa Drive. Possibly named for the city in the Central Valley, or for the Maricopa Indians of Arizona.

Mariposa Court. From the Spanish *mariposa*, butterfly.

Massol Avenue. Fenilen "Fen" Massol, one of the developers of the Almond Grove subdivision in 1887. (Fen's father, Florian, died a few years later.) A real estate and insurance agent, in partnership with O. B. Austin, jeweler.

Miles Avenue. John C. Miles, a native of Quebec who visited Los Gatos in the winter and subdivided this district with his friend Mr. Edelen in 1886.

Montebello Way (formerly Oak Street, Railroad Avenue). A common name in the west, derived from the Italian, "beautiful mountain." The current name was probably adopted after 1963 when the railroad tracks were removed.

Monterey Avenue. Refers to the nearby county, as do all the streets in the area: Santa Cruz, San Benito, San Mateo and Monterey are all California counties. The city of Monterey was the Mexican capital of Alta California until 1848, and is named for Monterrey in Spain, meaning *monte del rey*, or "mountain/forest of the king."

Monte Sereno. Spanish for calm woods. *Monte* means "bushes, brush, woods" and although it can mean "mountain," there is no evidence that it was used to refer to mountains except those covered with brush. The Americanos who named the peak west of Los Gatos Monte Sereno in the 1920s to add romantic appeal to the town probably wanted to believe that it meant "serene mountain." *See also* El Sombroso.

Montgomery Avenue. Named for John W. Montgomery, the Hoosier who opened the first harness shop in Los Gatos in 1874.

Mountain Charlie, or Charley. Named for Charles Henry McKiernan (1830-92), who settled in the Santa Cruz Mountains in 1851.

Mullen Avenue. The Mullen family sold the land for the grammar school (now Old Town) in 1880.

Newell Avenue. Unknown.

New York Avenue. The streets around the high school are named New York, Brooklyn and Chicago. Only New York is open at all times.

Nicholson Avenue. Augustine Nicholson, one of the developers of the Almond Grove in 1887 and owner of a 9-acre orchard in the town directory.

Oak Hill Way. Named for the hill between Tarantula Flats and Alpine, which was obviously named for the native trees (*Quercus agrifolia*, et. al.).

Oak Meadow. A seasonally marshy section of Los Gatos Creek, now tamed, approximately where Blossom Hill Road crosses. In the first half of the century, the area was the extreme north end of town and served as the garbage dump.

Ohlone Court. The native Coastanoan Indians are sometimes called the Ohlone (oh-lo-nee) tribe. Indian artifacts were found by the creek at Oak Meadow by the Nino and Forrest families who settled there in the 1880s and 1890s.

Oka Road. Unknown, probably a proper name.

Overlook Road. Refers to the view from the higher elevations, but the road winds higher than most—the private portion in Monte Sereno actually climbs several hundred feet higher than the public section.

Pageant Way (formerly Seanor). Named for the annual pageants produced at the site of the defunct Co-op Winery (south of today's civic center) 1920-47. Originally named for George Seanor, an early land owner and original trustee (1887-88).

Palm Avenue (formerly Santa Clara). Probably named for the popular palm trees which, while not native, seem to grow well in this climate. Santa Clara, the town, is named for the mission (1777) which honors Saint Clare of Assisi, co-founder of the Franciscan Order of Poor Clares.

Panighetti Way. Jack Panighetti, popular postmaster in the 1960s, belongs to a well-known local family.

Park Avenue. The road once led to the town park, dubbed Bunker Hill and rechristened Memorial Park after the Great War (1919).

Parr Avenue. Named for a family that owned several large tracts northwest of town at the turn of the century.

Pennsylvania Avenue. Named by Frank and Mary McCullagh, the subdividers, to remind them of their Philadelphia home. The upper portion of the road is listed as Orange Avenue on the 1895 Sanborn Map.

Peralta Avenue. Romantically named at or after the turn of the century for Sebastian Fabian Peralta, co-grantee of the original rancho. Peralta and his brother-in-law Hernandez profited little from their grant and both were dead when streets were named in their honor.

Petticoat Lane (formerly Fair Lane). Named by developer Effie Walton for her "Little Village" of shops.

Phillips Avenue. Unknown, possibly named for William H. Phillips, farmer, listed in the 1887 town directory.

Pollard Road. Probably named for an early land owner. A Claude Pollard was a high school student in 1898.

Quito Road. The Quito Rancho adjoined La Rinconada de los Gatos to the west. The name, which means "quits" in Spanish, may have been an error: the grant was also called Tito, after an Indian who occupied a portion of Mission Santa Clara.

Reservoir Road. Named for the cistern that originally ensured steady water pressure for Forbes Mill below. The covered reservoir still exists.

Roberts Road. Named for John J. Roberts, listed as a farmer in the 1887 town directory.

Rogers Street. Unknown, but likely a surname and possibly for Noah Garcelon Rogers, owner of the fruit packing plant at the corner of San Jose Road (Los Gatos Boulevard) and Los Gatos-Almaden Road.

Ross Creek. Perhaps named for John E. Ross, owner of 280 acres in the "Union district" (East Los Gatos) in 1858.

Royce Street. Named for Josiah Royce, mail agent and co-founder of the First Church of Christ Scientist congregation.

Samaritan Drive. Probably named for the Good Samaritan hospital, built in 1965.

San Benito Avenue. Refers to the adjacent county to the south, created in 1874, which honors St. Benedict, founder of the Benedictine Order. The 1895 Sanborn map names this street an extension of Tait Avenue, but street names north of Saratoga Road were later given their own identity.

San Mateo Avenue. Refers to the adjacent county to the northwest, created in 1856, which honors St. Matthew the apostle.

Santa Cruz Avenue. Roads in this area have traditionally been named for their destination, hence the road to the south is Santa Cruz Road. Before the towns of Alma and Lexington were obliterated by the reservoir construction, the road was sometimes known as Lexington Road.

Santa Cruz Avenue is divided by Main Street: South Santa Cruz extends south of Main.

Santa Rosa Drive. A fairly recent development named, with a fine sense of history, for James Forbes' brand of milled flour. Santa Rosa flour sacks, produced beginning 1854, are prized by collectors.

Saratoga Road. Also known as the Los Gatos-Saratoga Road, or Highway 9. The nearby town of Saratoga was named for Saratoga Springs, New York and developed as a resort after 1866.

Serra Court. One of the town's newest roads (1997), presumably named to honor Padre Junípero Serra.

Shannon Road. Named for Thomas Shannon, a forty-niner and lumberman who owned 160 acres around his redwood farmhouse in 1866.

Short Road. Possibly for A. C. Short, developer of Glen Ridge, or W. C. Short, town trustee and chairman (mayor) in 1916.

Simons Street. Named for Daniel Page Simons, a prominent local capitalist who invested his lumber money in projects such as the Mountain Spring Water Company and the Bean Spray Pump Company, which became FMC. Simons was twice elected to the Board of Trustees and served as chairman (mayor) from 1908 until his death in office in 1910.

Snell Road. Named for turn of the century property owner and printer Daniel Snell. The Snell family has lived on the property continuously since. It is not clear what relation, if any, they have to the family that named Snell Creek and Road in South San Jose.

Spreckles Drive. Subdivided by Richard and Anna Spreckles in the 1910s and 1920s as a bungalow park around their hospital (sanitarium). Distantly related to sugar baron Claus Spreckels. Richard took some part in the sugar operation, but spelled the surname differently.

Spring Street. Likely named for a spring which feeds the creek that runs between Johnson and Alpine Avenues.

Stacia Street. Reportedly named by subdivider Peter Johnson for one of his daughters in the mid-1880s.

Sund Avenue. Created with the Sund Land subdivision in the 1980s, the avenue runs through the 16-acre farm of Herman Sund, one of the founders of the town. The farmhouse he improved in 1884 has remained in the Sund family continuously.

Suview Drive. Unknown.

Tait Avenue. Named for Captain Magnus Tait, a Civil War veteran, one of the creators of the Almond Grove subdivision.

Topping Way. Possibly named for Harry S. Topping, a "vulcanizer" who lived on Glenridge in the 1910s.

Tourney Loop/Road. Named for Julius Tourney, an early landowner.

Turnstile Walk. The road, too narrow for carriages, leading from West Main to Fairview Plaza is known as "turnstile" today, meaning constricted, a bottleneck. It is not known if the name is original.

Twin Oaks Drive. As with all such names, one surmises that two prominent trees inspired the subdivider.

University Avenue (formerly School Street). Named to describe the "institution of higher learning" (grammar school) built in 1881 and continually improved until 1959. Perhaps it reflects some envy of Palo Alto, home to Stanford University beginning in 1891.

Vasona Lake, Park. Reportedly named c.1895 by local farmer Albert August Vollmer for a pony he had as a child. Vasona Junction was the stop on the Southern Pacific railroad before Los Gatos, at first a "flag stop" for Vollmer's daughter Agnes to get to work. (Source: Frazier O. Reed II, quoted on the Santa Clara County web site.)

Via. Vía Caballero = Rider/Horseman Road. Vía De Tesoros = Road of Treasure. Vía Encantada = Enchanted Road. Vía La Posada = The Lodging/Shelter Road. Vía Palomino, Pinto = Palomino, Pinto Road (refering to the variety of horse). Vía Vaquero = Cattle Road.

Via Santa Maria, Nina Court, Pinta Court. Named for the tiny fleet commanded by Christopher Columbus that "discovered" the western hemisphere in 1492.

Victory Lane. Likely named in 1919, when Bunker Hill Park was renamed Memorial Park, in patriotic support of our war effort "over there."

Villa Avenue. A true mystery. It may be a proper name, or it may refer to the Spanish for house or small town. One possibility is that the street is named for Pancho Villa, a Mexican revolutionary active on both sides of the border c. 1916.

Village Lane. Named by developer Effie Walton for her "Little Village" collection of shops.

Vista del Campo, Lago, Mar, Monte, Prado, Sierra. View of the countryside, lake, sea, forest, meadow, mountain range.

Walnut Avenue. Related to Chestnut, likely in reference to a neighborhood or the trees of the McCullagh's native Philadelphia.

Wheeler Avenue. Named for Charles H. Wheeler, a carpenter, home builder and developer, who served on the Board of School Trustees in 1902.

Whitney Avenue. Named for Elijah S. Whitney, an early landowner

Wilder Avenue. Named for Alphonse Eli Wilder, a banker, one of the developers of the Almond Grove district and a founder of the town. Like Daniel Simons, Wilder invested in John Bean's ventures and was well rewarded.

Winchester Boulevard. Named, probably posthumously, meaning after 1923, for the road's destination: the house of Sarah Winchester.

Wissahickon Avenue. Named by the nostalgic McCullaghs after their address in Philadelphia when they subdivided this district. It is variously given as the creek by which Frank McCullagh played as a child, or the county in which he grew or the street on which he lived.

Wood Road. Probably named for Colonel Erskine Scott Wood, a well-known lawyer, poet and Indian fighter who moved to town in the early 1920s and built an estate south of this road. The road accessed the rear portion of John Lyndon's lands which had previously been reached from Broadway.

Sources

Gudde, Erwin G. *California Place Names: The Origin and Etymology of Current Geographical Names*, 4th Ed. by William Bright. (Berkeley, Univ. of Ca. Press, 1998)

Langenscheidt's New College Spanish Dictionary (http://www.lhs-lt.de/en/products/bt1woerter.htm)

C Mayors

The town council was called the Board of Trustees prior to 1927, and the mayor was simply the Chairman of the Board.

1887	Palmer Perkins		1966	Egon Jensen
1888	John Weldon Lyndon		1968	John Michaelsen
1892	Peter Johnson		1969	Roland Perry
1894	Fenilen Massol (resigned)		1970	Dr. Charles DeFreitas
1897	Henry Schomberg		1971	Seymour Abrahams
1898	E. N. Davis		1972	Ruth Cannon (first woman)
1900	Thomas J. Davis		1973	Mark DiDuca
1902	James H. Lyndon		1974	John Lochner
1904	B. P. Shuler		1975	Egon Jensen
1906	T. E. Johns		1976	Ruth Cannon
1908	Daniel Page Simons		1977	Albert Smith
1910	George W. Turner		1978	Mardi Gualtieri
1912	R. R. Bell (resigned)		1979	John Lochner
1914	S. D. Balch		1980	Thomas Ferrito
1916	W. C. Short		1981	Peter Siemens
1918	J. J. Stanfield (resigned)		1982	Brent Ventura
1919	William F. Godfrey		1983	Thomas Ferrito
1920	Charles W. Gertridge		1984	Joanne Benjamin
1922	J. Walter Crider		1985	Terrence Daily
1924	Irving D. Mabie		1986	Brent Ventura
1926	George A. Green		1987	Eric Carlson
1928	A. H. Bell		1988	Joanne Benjamin
1930	Irving D. Mabie		1989	Thomas Ferrito
1932	Marcus Vertin		1990	Brent Ventura
1940	Carl S. Balch (resigned)		1991	Eric D. Carlson
1940	Stanley Mills		1992	Eric D. Carlson
1944	C. B. Spotswood		1993	Joanne Benjamin
1946	J. C. Adams		1994	Randy Attaway
1948	James F. Thompson (resigned)		1995	Patrick F. O'Laughlin
1951	Leroy H. Wright		1996	Randy Attaway
1952	Charles K. Gamble		1997	Joanne Benjamin
1954	Alberto E. Merrill		1998	Linda Lubeck
1962	John Lincoln		1999	Jan Hutchins

D Bibliography

Arbuckle, Clyde. *Clyde Arbuckle's History of San José*. San José: Memorabilia of San José, 1986. A very serious, complete work of some 535 pages, it includes various mentions of Los Gatos and the actions of some of its citizens with respect to San Jose.

Beal, Richard. *Highway 17: The Road to Santa Cruz,* 2nd Ed. Aptos: The Pacific Group, 1991. A marvelously entertaining guide to the highway through the mountains and the history of the towns along it, with significant specifics about Los Gatos and the construction of the freeway ISBN 0-9629974-0-4.

Bennett, Mardi. *Images of Long Ago: Photos, Postcards and "Pen Pictures of the Garden of the World": Los Gatos, Saratoga and Monte Sereno.* Los Gatos: Marben Associates, 1987. Former Mayor Mardi Gualtieri Bennett presents a treasury of antique photos illustrating the town and its people from the turn of the century and before.

Boutelle, Sara Holmes. *Julia Morgan, Architect.* New York: Abbeville Press, 1988. Perkins house pp. 157-160.

Broggie, Michael. *Walt Disney's Railroad Story: The Small-Scale Fascination The Led to a Full-Scale Kingdom.* Pasadena: Pentrex, 1997. ISBN 1-56342-006-6. Billy Jones is mentioned on pp. 173, 217, 219.

Bruntz, George G. *The History of Los Gatos, Gem of the Foothills.* Santa Cruz: Western Tanager Press, 1983. Originally published in 1971, this is the classic source of information on the history of the town. Bruntz based the book partly on material collected by Clarence F. Hamsher, to whom the book is dedicated.

Butler, Phyllis Filiberti. *Old Santa Clara Valley: A Guide to Historic Buildings from Palo Alto to Gilroy,* Rev. Ed. San Carlos: Wide World Publishing/Tetra, 1991. Originally published in 1975 by the Junior League of San Jose, the book includes a knowledgeable chapter on Los Gatos, including information about Hernandez and Peralta, but only details three buildings in town, two now destroyed, with 16 others mentioned in a supplement. ISBN 0-933174-81-0

Foote, Horace S., Ed. *Pen Pictures from the "Garden of the World"* Chicago: Lewis, 1888.

Gudde, Erwin G. *California Place Names: The Origin and Etymology of Current Geographical Names,* 4th Ed. Rev. and Enlarged by William Bright. Berkeley: University of California Press, 1998. 0-520-21316-5.

Hill, Andrew P. *Scenes Along the Line of the San Jose & Los Gatos Interurban Railroad.* San Jose: San Jose Historical Museum Association, 1994. A reprint of an album presented to the San Jose Chamber of Commerce at the time of the Railway's construction in 1904, with historical notes for each photograph.

Johnson, Kenneth M. *The New Almaden Quicksilver Mine.* Georgetown, CA: Talisman Press, 1963.

Lanyon, Milton and Laurence Bulmore. *Cinnabar Hills: The Quicksilver Days of New Almaden.* Los Gatos: Village Printers, 1967. A detailed history of the New Almaden quicksilver mine, including sketches of the interaction between James Forbes and the Barron & Forbes concern in Tepíc, Mexico.

Lazzarini, Jeanne. "Restoring a Town." *Victorian Homes* 13, Issue 5. Fall 1994. p54. A description of the rebuilding of certain Los Gatos homes after the 1989 earthquake.

Suggested Reading

The future of Los Gatos will be determined by its citizens. These two books will help.

Alexander, Christopher, et. al. *A Pattern Language.* New York: Oxford University Press, 1977.

Susanka, Susan with Kira Obolensky. *A Not So Big House: A Blueprint for the way we really live.* Newtown, CT: Taunton Press, 1998. ISBN: 1-56158-130-5.

Photographic Credits

Peter S. Conrad observed Los Gatos with several 35mm cameras, particularly a Ricoh FT1 using lenses from 28mm to 135mm, a tiny Olympus Stylus Epic, and a hand-restored 4x5 format 1939 Graflex Speed Graphic with a 135mm Wollensak lens. His work appears on both covers as well as pages *xii*, 9, 33, 35, 36, 38-39, 41, 44, 49, 50, 56-57, 69, 70, 72, 74-75, 79, 85, 86, 90, 95, 109, 113, 118-23, 125, 127, 131, 132, 136, 143, 146, 155, 156, 161.

Peggy Dallas contributed photographs on pages 115 and 149 and line art on page 107. Jonathan Dallas drew the illustration on page 100. Amy Konsterlie's watercolors appear on pages 7, 8 and 18.

Mary Tomasi-Dubois shared her photographs of Los Gatos activities used on pages 5 and 33. Kathryn Morgan took photographs just after the 1989 earthquake which are found on page 27. Thanks to John Pugh for the photographs of *Sieta Punto Uno* on pages 63-64.

The aerial photograph of downtown Los Gatos on page 28 is courtesy of Joel Avila of Hawkeye Aerial Photography.

Historical photographs on pages 5, 10, 15, 19, 31, 32, 34, 43, 47, 60, 68, 71 and 97 are from the Town of Los Gatos Library Collection. Once again, our deep appreciation to Gloria Grimes and her tireless staff.

The wonderful folks at the Jim Henson Company, particularly Jeff Cusson, made possible Gonzo the Great's appearance on page 104. Thanks to Dave Goelz and Ernest Patterson for the glossy.

All other photographs are by Alastair Dallas, using either a Kodak DC-210 digital camera or a Nikon N70 35mm camera with a Nikkor 28mm-70mm zoom lens. Future historians note: The modern photographs in this book (except Hawkeye) were all taken between May 1998 and July 1999.

Index